S0-BCG-786

YOU DON'T NEED
A TITLE TO BE A
LEADER

Also available by Mark Sanborn

The Fred Factor

YOU DON'T NEED A TITLE TO BE A LEADER

How Anyone, Anywhere, Can Make a Positive Difference

MARK SANBORN

BUSINESS
BOOKS

Published by Random House Business Books in 2006

1 3 5 7 9 10 8 6 4 2

Copyright © Mark Sanborn, 2006

Mark Sanborn has asserted his right under the Copyright, Designs
and Patents Act, 1988 to be identified as the author of this work.

This book is sold subject to the condition that it shall not, by way of trade
or otherwise, be lent, resold, hired out, or otherwise circulated without the
publisher's prior consent in any form of binding or cover other than that in which it
is published and without a similar condition including this condition being imposed
on the subsequent purchaser.

First published in the United Kingdom in 2006
by Random House Business Books.
First published in the United States in 2006
by Currency/Doubleday.

Random House Business Books
The Random House Group Limited
20 Vauxhall Bridge Road, London, SW1V 2SA

Random House Australia (Pty) Limited
20 Alfred Street, Milsons Point, Sydney,
New South Wales 2061, Australia

Random House New Zealand Limited
18 Poland Road, Glenfield
Auckland 10, New Zealand

Random House (Pty) Limited
Isle of Houghton, Corner of Boundary Road & Carse O'Gowrie
Houghton 2198, South Africa

Random House Publishers India Private Limited
301 World Trade Tower, Hotel Intercontinental Grand Complex,
Barakhamba Lane, New Delhi 110 001, India

The Random House Group Limited Reg. No. 954009

www.randomhouse.co.uk

A CIP catalogue record for this book is available from the British Library

Papers used by Random House are natural, recyclable products made from wood
grown in sustainable forests. The manufacturing processes conform to the
environmental regulations of the country of origin

ISBN 9781905211289 (from Jan 2007)
ISBN 1 9052 1128 7

Design by Tina Henderson

Printed and bound in Great Britain by
Bookmarque Ltd, Croydon, Surrey

To my parents
Leslie and Dorothy Sanborn
Who provided a strong foundation

To Dr. Earl ("Doc") Kantner
My mentor and friend

CONTENTS

Acknowledgments   ix

Introduction   xi

PART I: A LEADER IS . . .   1

They Didn't Need a Title to Be Leaders   3
   (and Neither Do You)

An Invitation to Greatness   10

Leaders Increase ROI   17

PART II: THE SIX PRINCIPLES OF LEADERSHIP   25

Principle 1: The Power of Self-Mastery   27

Principle 2: The Power of Focus   40

Principle 3: Power with People   50

Principle 4: The Power of Persuasive Communication   61

Principle 5: The Power of Execution   70

Principle 6: The Power of Giving   82

PART III: MAKING A POSITIVE DIFFERENCE   91

Leaving a Leadership Legacy   93

Mastering Leadership   103

ACKNOWLEDGMENTS

I am most appreciative of the many people who have offered stories and ideas for this book, particularly Dave and Sheri Hewitt, Scott McChrystal, and Julie Marks Miller.

Thank you to Andrew Stoller, Barbara Stammer, Bobby Merritt, Karen Wood, and Tony Schiller for allowing me to share their stories.

Thanks to Susan Suffes and John Bolin for their contributions to the manuscript.

I especially want to thank my editor, Roger Scholl, for his expert collaboration, and my publisher, Michael Palgon, for his exceptional support.

My literary agent, Sealy Yates, and strategic advisor, Kevin Small, are both enormously skilled at what they do and also great friends. Thanks, guys.

My family means the world to me, so thank you Darla, Hunter, and Jackson for your love and support. I love you more than you can ever imagine.

Finally, but most important, I thank God for His blessings. The sentiment of John Newton's classic hymn summarizes my life: Through many dangers, toils and snares, I have already come. Grace has brought me safe thus far and grace will lead me home . . .

INTRODUCTION

Recently, the vice president of a multinational technology company I know needed someone on his team to lead a mission-critical project. It wasn't enough to find someone who would do a good job. He needed a leader who would do a great job.

After careful thought and consideration, he approached a colleague, whom I'll call Bob, who was considered an up-and-comer. Bob had demonstrated tremendous potential. His work on previous projects had been exemplary. As past performance is one of the best indicators of future performance, the VP decided to sit down with him.

After explaining the project and what he wanted Bob to do, the VP extended an invitation to him to lead the project.

After a brief pause, Bob responded, "I assume you'll make me a director if I take this on."

His unexpected response caused the VP to pause. What were Bob's real motivations? Was he a person driven by the need to contribute, or the need to gain? Would he act in the best interest of the organization, or only himself? After brief hesitation, the VP explained that the title change didn't go with the assignment. Furthermore, he went on, given Bob's concern, maybe Bob wasn't the right person to lead the project. The VP withdrew his offer and went back to the drawing board. After more deliberation, he came up with an alternative candidate. The person who came to mind was a woman, Gail, who had also shown great promise. Gail wasn't actually a member of his team—in fact, she acted in a freelance capacity. But the VP knew Gail's can-do attitude and strong people and problem-solving skills were what was needed. Despite her lack of an official position within the company, the VP decided to ask Gail to lead the project.

Given his experience with Bob, he approached her with some apprehension. After extending the offer, he added: "I want you to know that if you accept this challenge, and succeed, I can't automatically make you a director."

Gail didn't even hesitate. "That's all right," she said. *"I don't need a title to be a leader."*

LEADERSHIP IS INFLUENCE

I couldn't have said it any better. You don't need a title to be a leader in life. And the simple fact of having a title won't make you a leader.

I've found that everyone has the opportunity to lead, every day. It doesn't matter what your position is, or how long you've worked at your job, whether you help to run your family, a PTA committee, or a Fortune 1000 company. Anyone at any level can learn to be a leader and help to shape or influence the world around them.

Do you shape your life and career?
Do you affect the quality of others' experiences?
Do you inspire or influence others?

Do you work to achieve specific goals by working with or
coordinating the efforts of others?

If you answered "yes" to any of these questions whether you
realize it or not, you are a leader.

Leadership expert John Maxwell describes leadership as *positive influence*. That is the most simple and elegant definition of
leadership I know.

In my experience, people lead for different reasons. The one
thing they do have in common is passion—passion for life and
for what they do. It's an attitude that applies in spades to West
Point's Karen Wood. For more than twenty years, Karen has
worked as an aide to the adjutant general.

Had it not been for Karen's dogged perseverance, Donald
Stewart, a World War II veteran, might not have gotten the
recognition he deserved for his service as a medic on the front
lines in 1943. He had saved the lives of countless soldiers while
under fire himself. When Karen discovered that Mr. Stewart
had never been awarded a Bronze Star for his valor and courage,
she worked tirelessly behind the scenes to make the award presentation a reality. Given the veteran's advanced age, Karen
knew it was critical to get him the award as quickly as possible.
She found a way to cut through the red tape and make it
happen, as she had orchestrated so many important events at
West Point.

For years, Karen's own dream had been to become a protocol officer. But rather than interviewing for the position, she
simply worked as hard, and passionately, and selflessly in her role
as aide as she knew how, consistently giving her best efforts to

the officers she worked with. The higher-ups at the Academy were well aware of her exemplary performance and leadership, and her qualifications for the job. Given that, you won't be surprised to learn that Karen was recently promoted. She is now a protocol officer, working for the superintendent of the Academy.

"I believe that if you give 110 percent in your work it will come back tenfold," she says. As the single parent of a fifteen-year-old daughter, this is the work ethic she tries to teach her daughter, as well.

"Life is what you make of it. The more you put into it, the more it reflects back on you."

HOW DOES A LEADER ACT?

What are the key characteristics of titled and untitled leaders? They:

- Believe they can positively shape their lives and careers.
- Lead through their relationships with people, as opposed to their control over people.
- Collaborate rather than control.
- *Persuade* others to contribute, rather than order them to.
- Get others to follow them out of respect and commitment rather than fear and compliance.

THE LEADERSHIP TEST

Despite popular myth, leaders—whether titled or untitled—aren't born. They *learn* how to lead. The real test of leadership is: If you had no title or ability to reward or penalize others, could you still get them to follow you?

You may be unaware of just how much of a leader you already are. You may be part of a large group of people I call the "undertitled." In other words, your title doesn't reflect all that you do or accomplish. If that describes you, don't let your lack of a title hold you back. You *are* a leader. (Conversely, we all know "leaders" who have impressive titles but who are anything but leaders.)

For those of you who would like to have a greater impact on those around you, this book will help show you how to *become* a leader.

One last thing. There are plenty of books written about leadership with a capital *L*. The focus of this book is on "little *l*" leadership—whether you are a clerk or an accountant, or a manager, or a salesperson, or a small-business owner. It is about the small things each of us can do every day to positively influence our customers, our colleagues, our friends, and our communities.

You aspire to lead if you want to:

- take control of your life
- make your organization better
- seize new opportunities
- improve the service your customers receive
- influence others to be their best
- solve problems
- contribute to the betterment of others
- make the world a little better

And you don't need a title to do it.

PART I

A LEADER IS . . .

THEY DIDN'T NEED A TITLE
TO BE LEADERS
(AND NEITHER DO YOU)

ANDREA

A famous politician once said, "The longer the title, the less important the job." If that's true, then Andrea Stoller has a very important job indeed. Just ask anyone who has had contact with her at the school where she has worked for the past fifteen years.

Andrea is not a licensed teacher. In fact, Andrea Stoller has no real "title" at all. What does she do? Nearly everything. She wears dozens of hats, including that of accountant, nurse, receptionist, secretary, admissions coordinator, supply coordinator, and counselor. And although she doesn't have an official title, her favorite is the one that nearly 200 students give to her every year. They call her "Mom."

I'm convinced that at the heart of every successful organization is a title-less person or persons just like Andrea.

One day, Andrea received a phone call informing her that one of the students, coming home from soccer practice, had been in a fatal car accident. When the teenage girl had gotten out of her car, an older man driving another car accidentally hit her, killing her instantly. The tragedy was devastating for the girl's family and classmates, as well as for the young man she had been dating at the time, Simon.

After the accident, Simon sunk into a deep depression, avoiding people and falling behind in his schoolwork. It seemed as though he would become collateral damage in the tragedy. Andrea spotted the signs of his depression and attempted to befriend him. She offered to help him with his class work and tutor him, despite the fact that she didn't have a teacher's degree.

At graduation, everyone applauded when Simon walked to the dais to give the commencement address. In his speech, he specifically thanked Andrea for helping him to graduate. Today, the young man who nearly lost hope when he lost his high school sweetheart is a nationally recognized skateboarder. He regularly encourages other students, just as Andrea encouraged him.

Given Andrea's stature at the school, it's not surprising that many students choose to use one of their class electives to serve as office aides with her. Not only do they learn good office skills from her, but they know they will receive much-prized one-on-one time with her. She listens to them, advises them, and cares for them when they are sick or need help. In fact, she has such a kind, understanding heart that even parents have come to her with their own problems (divorce, issues with their kids, etc.).

One summer the local junior high burned down. As a result, the school where Andrea worked needed to create more space quickly to house extra students. The school decided to add several modular buildings to its campus.

With necessary last-minute construction and repairs to be done, Andrea and her husband worked late into the evening for weeks, staying until midnight at times, in order to be ready for the building inspectors so school could open on time.

Andrea even found a temporary location for those classes whose rooms were not yet approved by the time the school year started—the church she attends offered to let the school use their facility for several weeks. And, as a result of Andrea's "negotiations," the school paid very little to rent the facilities.

Andrea Stoller still doesn't have a title. But she leads and influences others in significant ways every day.

WHAT GOOD IS A TITLE?

In today's world, much is made of a person's title. Yet little actual power exists in a title alone.

I once did a survey on my Web site about the reasons people had for acting as leaders. One woman replied, "I want to be Ruler of the Universe someday, and figure being a leader at my company is a good place to start."

Her wry sense of humor underscores the appeal of titles; they suggest that one has achieved power, position, prestige, and privilege.

But are titles really that powerful? What does a title *really* confer?

An article in the *New York Times* described a corporate communications officer at Amtrak whose title had been changed from "Vice President" to "Chief." But the title change wasn't the result of a promotion. When the company reduced the number of VPs from eighty-five to ten, he was given the new title to make him feel better—he was one of the select few in the company to hold such a position. What kind of impact did the new title have on the people under him? "It meant absolutely nothing," the new chief acknowledged.

Sometimes it is easier to give an employee an important-sounding title than pay him or her more (although, according to one survey, 85 percent of people would pass up a bigger title for a 10 percent increase in pay). Marc Cenedella, president and chief executive of TheLadders.com, an executive job-search site, says, "You're never going to get hired based on your title, in and of itself. A job title's more useful internally to your company and for how you feel you're viewed."

In other words, a title is not a job description. There are some things that a title can suggest, like having responsibility for others and getting results. It can't, however, specifically define what a person *does*. Titles are broad brushstrokes.

In fact, when it comes to true power, titles are frequently misleading. Even at the level of CEO, a company head who is disliked can be all but ignored by those under her or him, while a respected employee with a lower title can wield significant influence on what others do and how quickly they do it.

It's impossible for a title or an organizational chart to reflect all the many people who act as leaders or exert leadership throughout the organization. That is why I call such people "nontitled leaders." They may or may not have direct responsibility to lead others, yet every day they influence and lead those around them.

The bottom line is, influence and inspiration come from the person, not the position.

AN ARMY OF LIONS

Philip of Macedonia, the father of Alexander the Great, said, "An army of deer led by a lion is more to be feared than an army of lions led by a deer." That may be true, but I've come to believe that Philip missed the bigger point: *An army of lions led by a lion is to be feared most of all, for it is unstoppable.*

What's more powerful than having strong, effective leadership at the top of your organization? Having an organization of lions where *everyone* leads.

At any Toyota plant, every employee on the line has the authority and responsibility to shut down the line at any time they feel necessary. Quality control and problem solving aren't left to the titled managers. A woman who spots a problem is expected to lead by calling attention to it rather than allowing it to slip through and become an imperfection on a dealer's lot or owner's driveway.

My friend Susan told me a story about the best receptionist she ever met, a woman who served as the "front person" at the company where she worked. On her desk was a sign: RECEPTIONISTVILLE. POPULATION: 1. If you asked her what her title was, she'd respond, "Intergalatic Empress." She took herself lightly, but her job seriously. She was a leader for the company as its first point of contact.

A cable TV installer I met in one of my seminars prided himself on the many value-added services he provided customers when he worked in their homes, including setting the clock to the correct time on their electronic devices and showing them how to use features that confused them. He didn't consider himself an installer, but a "home-entertainment consultant."

A volunteer at a nonprofit, filling in by answering the phones, took a phone call from a disgruntled donor. The donor felt unappreciated. The volunteer was able to communicate the gratitude of the organization for the donor's previous support, thereby regaining his loyalty. In the end, the volunteer's sincerity and belief in the work of the organization convinced the donor to increase his support.

LEADERSHIP LARGE AND SMALL

Many suffer from the misconception that leadership is about large, sweeping acts of history: Abraham Lincoln and the Emancipation Proclamation, Churchill and his "Blood, Sweat and Tears" speech during the Second World War.

Yes, those history-making events certainly marked extraordinary acts of leadership and courage. But what we don't always realize is that each of our daily actions and efforts have significant impact, as well. Rosa Parks had no idea of the impact she would have on history when she refused to give up her seat to a white man on that bus in Montgomery, Alabama. Yet her actions and courage changed the course of our nation's history.

When you do your job—any job—with initiative and determination to make a positive difference, you become a leader.

Sandra Dowling, the founder of Pappas School for homeless students in Phoenix, explains the power of individual leadership this way: "When a new teacher comes to the school, I tell them, 'If you went into teaching to make a difference, I want to welcome you. But at this school, you won't *make* a difference; you will *be* the difference.'"

AN INVITATION TO GREATNESS

If you're big enough for your dream,
your dream isn't big enough for you.
—Erwin Raphael McManus, pastor and author

WHO IS A LEADER?

One day, my assistant informed me over the intercom, "There is a Cadet Green on line two. I think you'll want to talk to him."

That was my introduction to Cadet Shawn Green, U.S. Air Force Academy.

The Air Force Academy had been in the papers a great deal lately for various challenges it was facing, and none of the recent news had been positive.

Shawn Green called me to tell me he had read my first book, *The Fred Factor*. He believed the book offered a message that needed to be shared at the Academy. So he took the initiative to call me out of the blue to ask if I would be willing to come and speak. "I'm just a person who wants to make things better," he told me.

This exceptional individual was undaunted by the

challenge of contacting people he didn't know who he thought could help. He couldn't afford to pay the people he was contacting to appear. In fact, he actually had to get official approval for us to appear for free. Cadet Green didn't have a title, but he was certainly a leader.

As a result of his bold request, both bestselling author Stephen Covey and I came to speak to the graduating class of freshman cadets. Meeting so many of the best of the best who were determined to serve their country was a memorable experience, one that I will not soon forget.

People who lead—whether or not they have a title—strive to make things better.

We all want to have an impact on the world around us. No one wants to be blown sideways in life by forces they can't control. Part of growing up is figuring out how much influence we have over our environment, from parents to friends, from school to careers.

Our choices in life have a huge impact on the kind of education we get, the kinds of jobs we land, the relationships we develop and become involved in, and the quality of the lives we live. The desire to influence the world around us is what real leadership is all about.

DO YOU THINK YOU MAKE A DIFFERENCE?

When you first look in the mirror in the morning, do you say to yourself, "Today, I'm going to change the world!"?

Probably not.

And yet we *do* change history every day, not just for ourselves but for our families, communities, employers, and country. Some of the ways we effect change are significant: landing a huge account, raising money for charity, helping to coach a youth soccer team. Others are small: letting someone merge ahead of us in traffic, taking an interest in a colleague who needs someone to listen. But none are trivial.

I'm not suggesting that simple acts of courtesy in and of themselves constitute acts of leadership. Yet leaders, untitled or otherwise, realize the extraordinary impact they can have on others and the world around them. They consciously choose to exercise their abilities, skills, and knowledge to help make a difference.

WHAT IS IT YOU WANT?

Professor of sociology and speaker Tony Campolo claims that if you ask most parents what they want for their children, they will say they want their children to be happy.

Campolo goes on to say that he grew up in a home where his father didn't *care* if he was happy. You see, his father wanted *more* for his children than just to be happy. He wanted each of them to be good, to be an ethical person who makes a positive contribution. Sometimes that requires hard work and self-sacrifice, putting another's needs ahead of your own. These are things that might not, in the short term, make us "happy." But they do help us to do good and make a difference. Being happy is enviable, but being good is truly admirable. It requires character, integrity, and perseverance.

Sometimes being "good" isn't aiming high enough. As Erwin McManus, the pastor of Mosaic Church in Los Angeles, said, "We spend so much time worrying about our kids being good—not breaking the rules, getting into trouble, and basically behaving—that *we often forget to invite them to be great.*"

In fact, I define true leadership as "an invitation to greatness that we extend to others." There is a catch, though. We can't give what we don't have. We can't extend an invitation we haven't already accepted.

At a recent convention, a member of the association sponsoring the event volunteered to work as backstage manager and assist with everything that happened behind the scenes at the general sessions. Because Rick was busy preparing between general sessions, he gave up the chance to attend most of the sessions during the conference. He didn't receive any payment, other than the appreciation of the association leaders, and he still paid a full registration fee for his attendance.

He was an example of one of the many who serve as untitled leaders, who handle the necessary but often unglamorous jobs that need to be done.

Volunteers for important or high-profile tasks are never in short supply. While I don't want to shortchange the importance of "the big show," I am even more impressed by the leaders who know what must be done behind the scenes to make the big show happen. They take on difficult and time-consuming assignments not because they want to be praised or noticed but just because those tasks have to be done. As a result, everyone benefits.

The reality is that we all work "backstage" in our lives at times. Real leaders bring the same commitment to excellence to whatever they do, whether on the stage or behind it.

DON'T CONFUSE LEADERSHIP WITH FAME

Recently, the Discovery Channel aired a four-part special on the top 100 greatest Americans. Matt Lauer hosted the show each week for one month; half a million nominations were gathered online. At the end, the top twenty-five Americans were announced. The results were what most people would call a mixed bag: Among those on the list were Abraham Lincoln and Arnold Schwarzenegger, Bill Clinton and Billy Graham, Thomas Jefferson and Tom Cruise, Walt Disney and John F. Kennedy, Dr. Phil and Michael Moore. The mixture of historically great leaders and entertainers like Michael Jackson and real estate mogul Donald Trump begs the question: What do we think "greatness" is?

In my opinion, fame is based on what we *get* in life, but true greatness is based on what we *give* in life. It is contribution through action.

BARBARA STAMMER

Barbara Stammer's career plans changed when she was nineteen years old. At the time, she was attending college with the intention of becoming a schoolteacher. Then the guy she planned to marry broke off the engagement and she left college to pick up the pieces and find herself. "All my plans were down the tubes," Barbara recalls. "I remember thinking 'What will I do with my life?'"

As luck would have it, a budding restaurateur named Bobby Merritt was hiring. Only months earlier, he had been employed driving a bread truck. Then he had a bad accident that changed his life forever. "I was in and out of hospitals over the next few years and was left with a permanent disability," says Bobby.

While recovering and considering how to take care of his wife and three small children, he found a help-wanted ad in the local newspaper. A restaurant chain called Sonic was looking for a managing partner in Las Cruces, New Mexico. And that's how Bobby got started in the restaurant business.

Barbara was the first employee Bobby hired. He knew her mother, who ran a commissary at a military base, from his bread truck route and her mother's own attitude and loyalty had always impressed him. As he expected, these traits run in the family. Barbara's can-do attitude and enthusiasm quickly helped her to learn the Sonic business.

Merritt bought out his original partners and started expanding. In December, as he prepared to open up a new drive-in restaurant, he asked Barbara to help train the crew. It was the first time she had helped to train someone else. "Soon I was ordering equipment and uniforms and doing everything necessary to get ready for a new opening." She discovered that not only was she good at doing *her* job, she was good at teaching others, as well.

"Barb," Bobby remembers, "was high-energy. She always wanted to make whatever she did better."

With her strong work ethic and sense of integrity, Barbara treated the business as if it were her own. Her passion and sense of responsibility made her a stellar employee, and Bobby continued to increase her responsibilities.

Yet she didn't have a title. Nor did she have one for the next fifteen or twenty years, until one day "Sonic Corporate said we had grown so much we needed an org chart," she said, laughing. "Bobby stopped by my office and asked me if I would like to be president. I said I would think about it. I never got back to him, but at the next company convention he announced that I had agreed to be president!"

Barbara Stammer helped Bobby Merritt build the largest Sonic franchise system in the United States, with 5,500 employees, 130-plus stores, $160 million in revenues, and some of the highest performance numbers in the business. And Barbara didn't need a title to do it (although she came to earn one in time).

BEING A LEADER

Genuine leaders make things better not just for themselves but for others, whether or not their contribution results in financial reward or popular recognition. A few leaders achieve both fame and greatness, and we read about them in history books. But most of the people I think of as leaders are untitled people like Barbara Stammer; they achieve greatness by working quietly in their organizations and communities, in their own lives, and in helping those around them.

In the following chapters, you'll learn what *you* can do to be a leader in life and at work, whether titled or untitled.

LEADERS INCREASE ROI

To affect the quality of the day,
that is the highest of arts.
—Henry David Thoreau

ROI

Several years ago, I experienced an unfortunate breakdown in service with my insurance broker, whom I had used for many years. It was serious enough for me to escalate my complaint to one of the owners of the company. To my surprise, he expressed complete disregard for my situation. Offended, I decided to take my business elsewhere.

But I never did. What held me back was what I call "the hassle factor." I had several policies in place that were brokered by this insurance provider, and changing policies would cause more hassle than it was worth. I figured when each policy came up for renewal, I would shop for another insurance company at that time.

As fate would have it, something happened to one of my vehicles. In order to submit a claim, I was forced to call the brokerage company I had come to dislike so greatly.

The customer-service rep who previously handled my

account was gone, and the woman who drew my number was named Theresa.

I was polite but direct when she and I spoke. "Look," I said, "I imagine you can tell from my records that my experiences with your firm haven't been good. If it weren't for the hassle of switching policies in effect, I'd take all my business elsewhere and never do business with your company again. It isn't anything personal. This is the first time you and I have spoken. But you need to know where I'm coming from."

Theresa listened attentively and floored me with her response. "Mr. Sanborn," she said, "I don't know all that happened to you, but I can understand that you are upset about your past dealings with us. I can't control what happened in the past, but I assure you of this: If you continue to do business with us, I will personally assist you and make sure that nothing like that happens again."

That was several years ago. My policies came up for renewal, but I never left, thanks to the personal leadership exhibited by Theresa.

In her thoughtful, direct way, Theresa increased what I call ROI: No, not her company's "return on investment" (although she did that, too). I'm referring to Relationships, Outcomes, and Improvements.

Leadership is intimately linked to service. I often relate stories of people who lead by increasing or improving the service they provide to a customer. But these are not "customer service" stories per se.

Customer service is about doing what you are supposed to do to help a customer. When you act as a leader, you go above and beyond the call of duty. Years of experience have convinced me that everyone who leads is involved in service leadership.

When we lead, everything we do is geared toward creating some kind of positive outcome, whether improving income, relationships, spiritual life, health, or career. But leadership can be about dollars and cents (sense) as well.

THE $1,500 BEVERAGE

I was famished. I had fasted for a medical procedure that was scheduled for early morning; in addition to being hungry, I was dying for my morning jump start of caffeine. Fortunately, there was a Starbucks located just around the corner from the hospital, so I picked up a cappuccino to go.

There was a popular deli nearby. I knew from previous experience that the food was good, so I parked and went inside with my just-started Starbucks cappuccino. "One for breakfast," I said to the hostess.

Seeing my Starbucks cup, she rather sternly replied, "We don't allow outside food or beverages in the restaurant. You'll either have to down it or leave it at the counter."

I wasn't about to discard my three-dollar cappuccino, so I decided to take my coffee and money elsewhere.

Her curt challenge to my not-purchased-there coffee felt like a personal rebuke. I could empathize with a business owner who wanted to sell his or her own coffee, but I had already purchased mine elsewhere. I was more than willing to spend $10 for breakfast, but the restaurant, by requiring that I dispense of my recently purchased Starbucks cappuccino, ended up with nothing and lost me permanently as a customer.

Upset at how I was treated, I called my brother Shawn, who is a successful restaurant owner and operator. After explaining the scenario, I asked for his opinion on what had happened. He saw an easy solution:

"She should have said, 'We don't allow outside food or beverages, so let me pour your drink into one of our cups after I seat you.' No competitor's coffee cup would be on the table, you would keep your beverage, and they would get to keep the money you spent on breakfast."

Why didn't she think about that? Because she was blindly enforcing the restaurant's policy without much regard for the effect it had on its customers. By not choosing to lead or influence the situation positively so that we both could win, she influenced negatively and lost a customer. This kind of behavior happens every day in business and in life: The woman who refuses to shop at a department store because she has been ignored or treated rudely. The harassed mother who decides not to volunteer her time to the local Girl Scout troop because she's constantly asked to do things at the last minute with no time to prepare. In each case, someone dropped the leadership ball.

One simple sentence could have earned that deli $1,500 a year—the cost of my breakfast three times a week over the next year. That would have been a pretty good return on investment.

GENUINE LEADERS LOOK FOR WAYS TO LEAD

For years a first-rate hotel tried to identify returning guests before they presented themselves to the front desk. Of course, the hotel's computer records would indicate if a guest had stayed before, but was there a way for staff to acknowledge a guest before he or she made it to reception?

An ingenious bellcap came up with a clever idea. When he greeted each guest arriving by car, taxi, or shuttle, he would say, "Welcome to the hotel. Have you stayed with us before?" If they responded in the affirmative, he would, as he handed them off to someone to help with their baggage, tug on his left ear. His ear tug signaled a returning guest, who could then be treated as such by hotel employees even before checking in.

Here is another example of someone who acted as a leader on his own initiative. A friend of mine was staying in the Omni hotel in San Diego when he discovered he didn't have any collar stays for his dress shirts. About to go into an important meeting, he didn't have time to go shopping for this common but sometimes difficult-to-find item.

He expressed his dilemma to a hotel employee, who, after suggesting several alternatives, came up with the perfect solution. Since the plastic cards used as room keys are approximately the same thickness as a collar stay, the innovative employee cut up a room key card to create custom collar stays for him.

Of course, my friend was delighted—both with the solution to his problem and the ingenuity of this nontitled leader. That small improvement made an enormous difference to my friend's experience.

STORE GREETERS, BLENDED BEVERAGES, AND COFFEE CUP SLEEVES

Did you know the person who suggested the idea of a store greeter that has become such an important part of the Wal-Mart brand wasn't a manager; he was a cashier—a nontitled leader.

Here is another example of how a small improvement can make an enormous difference. In the late 1980s in Portland, Jay Sorensen ordered a cup of coffee at a drive-through. Although wrapped in a napkin, it was still hot enough to cause him to drop it in his lap. In the early '90s, as the Starbucks-driven coffee craze was taking off, he watched over and over again at the way customers carefully held their coffee cups, even when "double-cupped," because the beverages were so hot. It's a phenomenon many of us experienced, a source of irritation we endured but never thought to address. Using supplies at home, Jay designed a cardboard sleeve to solve the problem. It became known as a Java Jacket, and the company he formed to make them today sells about 700 million units annually. Again, small improvements lead to big results.

Another untitled leader is the Starbucks store manager who invented the Frappuccino. When CEO Howard Schultz found out about the experiment and tasted it himself, he didn't like it. However, plenty of other people did. So he tested and refined it, and rolled it out in 1995. Within three years, it had generated $100 million in revenue for the company. That is the power of untitled leadership. The manager wasn't responsible for creating more drinks or expanding Starbucks' coffee line. But he did it anyway, just because it seemed like a good idea.

TAKING THE LEAD

In the early years of our nation, a pastor named Russell Conwell noticed that Charles Davies, a young man who was a member of his church, seemed troubled after an evening service.

Being a sensitive and perceptive person, Conwell asked Charlie what was wrong. Charlie explained that he didn't make much money and had little potential for earning more. In addition, he had to take care of his mother. He had longed to become a pastor but didn't hold much hope of getting the education he needed. What could he do?

Pastor Conwell responded immediately: "Come to me one evening a week and I will begin teaching you myself." Davies asked if he could bring a friend, and Conwell told him to bring as many as he wanted.

Conwell taught six young men that first evening. Forty attended by the third session. Before long, other educators offered to help teach. They rented a room, then later bought some buildings. That is how, as Gregory Dixon writes in his biography of Russell Conwell, Temple University was founded.

But Russell Conwell had a title, didn't he? Yes, he was a pastor, and a lawyer and entrepreneur. He was also the author of a bestselling book called *Acres of Diamonds*. He was considered perhaps the greatest motivational speaker of his day.

But he wasn't an educator or academic. He didn't have a teaching degree or experience running an educational institute. Nonetheless, he founded a university. And the reason he did it? He was responding to a need.

Conwell explained it best himself: "Greatness . . . consists in doing great deeds with little means and the accomplishment of vast purposes from the private ranks of life. To be great at all, one must be great here, now, in Philadelphia." Or Denver, or Cleveland, or wherever you currently reside.

Can you think of a relationship that needs to be strengthened or improved? Can you recall an outcome that might have turned out differently if you had taken the lead? And what about that idea you've been carrying around in your head that will improve your product or service? These are your opportunities to increase ROI: Relationships, Outcomes, and Improvements.

PART II

THE SIX PRINCIPLES OF LEADERSHIP

THE POWER OF
SELF-MASTERY

The hardest victory is over self.

—ARISTOTLE

LEADING FROM WITHIN

Mattie, whose full name was Matthew Joseph Thaddeus Stepanek, was born in Washington, D.C., on July 17, 1990. He had a serious disability, dysautonomic mitochondrial myopathy. His disability interrupted automatic functioning like breathing, heart rate, blood pressure, and body temperature. As a result, he needed a breathing tube and ventilator; a tube was inserted into the top of his heart to administer medicines and IV fluids. Mattie was confined to a wheelchair. He died just weeks before his fourteenth birthday.

But that didn't stop him from becoming a bestselling author and poet, an award-winning speaker, and a recognized advocate for disability and peacemaking. All five of his Heartsongs series of poetry books were *New York Times* bestsellers. Before he became confined to his wheelchair, he had earned a first-degree black belt in the martial art hapkido.

Despite the challenges of his situation, he was a practical joker who lived by the philosophy "Remember to play after every storm." Mattie's enthusiasm for life was infectious, and people around the world were touched not just by the poetry he wrote and the words he spoke, but by the example of how he lived his life.

Mattie refused to allow circumstances to control his destiny. Rather, he mastered his circumstances.

The fact is, all leadership begins with self-mastery. You can't lead others until you can first lead yourself.

As Mahatma Gandhi said, "Be the change you wish to see in the world." To truly lead, and make a difference in the world, you must always start with yourself.

I've rarely met a person who didn't want to make more money, be a better spouse or parent, become a better employer, take a more active role in their community or in a group. But I've also rarely met anyone—and I include myself—who has accomplished this to the degree she or he is capable.

Few of us live our lives to our full potential.

AN OBLIGATION OR AN OPPORTUNITY

Earlier in my career, while I was building my business, I became increasingly involved in association leadership. I reached a point where I felt so overwhelmed with the obligations this entailed that when the phone rang I didn't want to answer it. I knew I had to make a change.

So, drawing from the examples of the world's great leaders, I reframed how I saw my work and life. I began to see what happened to me as an *opportunity* rather than an *obligation*. And it made all the difference. Now when the phone rings, I respond to each call as an opportunity to serve, earn, learn, influence, network, encourage, or teach. The difference isn't in the caller or the purpose for the call; the difference is in my response.

I now keep a sign over my desk that reads: "Obligation or Opportunity."

How do you live life? As an obligation, or as an opportunity? Those who see life as an obligation want the task at hand to be done with as quickly as possible, with little regard to the outcome.

The people who change the world around them—for themselves, their companies, communities, and families—rarely act from a sense of obligation. In fact, the people who act as leaders almost always act from a sense of incredible opportunity. They don't interact with the world around them because they *have* to. They do so because they *want* to.

I doubt that Mother Teresa woke up even one morning and complained, "Oh, Lord, not more lepers!" She did some of the hardest work on the planet, yet she seemed to have more fun doing it than we do sitting in plush, air-conditioned offices.

When we feel harried and pressured, we tend to look at our circumstances as obligations, and obligations, by their nature, are oppressive. They are things we have to do, whether we want to or not. That sense of obligation is rarely a motivating force. On the other hand, those who lead effectively tend to view such circumstances as opportunities. They tend to be happier because they realize they can make something good out of a situation or a circumstance that others would bemoan or at best tolerate. Simply put, leaders, titled or not, believe that how we live our lives is a choice.

MONEY VS. MEANING

The *Wall Street Journal* recently reported that 80 percent of line workers and 50 percent of executives are dissatisfied with their lives at work. Many people feel a disconnect between the meaning and purpose of their lives. According to Barna Research, a research company in Indianapolis that specializes in issues of church and faith, nearly one out of every two people is trying to figure out their purpose in life.

Why do you go to work in the morning? Is it to make money, to pay the mortgage, put the kids through school, and make the car payment? Most people, when asked that question, would say they go to work to earn a living.

There is nothing inherently wrong with that answer. But it is far from the only reason to go to work. Sure, everyone needs money to survive. The problem occurs when making money is separated from giving purpose and meaning to our lives.

The challenge for anyone is to make a *life* while making a living. That means making money and meaning during the workday. Then what you do on the weekends or evenings becomes icing on the cake.

In psychology circles, connecting to something beyond the self, and helping others find fulfillment and realize their potential, is called self-transcendence. If you've taken an entry-level psychology class, you may recall that Abraham Maslow, one of the pioneers of psychology, placed transcendence at the top of his "hierarchy of needs." But the fact is that real leaders, whether they have a title or not, transcend personal needs and interests regularly in their effort to benefit others.

Genuine, authentic leadership infuses meaning into your life, because you know that your efforts count and that you are serving the needs of others as well as your own.

THE ROAD LESS TRAVELED

In his classic poem "The Road Not Taken," Robert Frost talks about two diverging roads he encountered in the woods. By taking the one less traveled, his life was changed. Frost's point was that taking the same path as everyone else will only get you average or mediocre results. To be unique, to contribute something new, one needs to take a different course—his or her own.

People who lead are willing to do the hard work of finding out what their unique gifts and contributions are, then doing the even harder work of designing their lives around them. Without question, it is far easier to take the beaten path and enjoy the security of conformity. Many people hold back from acting like leaders because they don't want to be the nail that sticks out and gets hammered in. So they give in and become one of the crowd.

When you act as a leader, you exercise control over your life and help to influence and inspire those around you. Relinquishing control of your life to external situations, circumstance, and culture is the opposite. To act as a leader, you must constantly ask yourself, Who is in charge of my life? Who is in charge of *me*?

THINK LIKE A LEADER

Management guru Tom Peters claims that the worst thing that can happen to us as leaders is to exhaust our intellectual capital. We must constantly refresh ourselves by gathering new information and thinking critically about the information we receive.

Thinking about life's issues is vital in being a leader, to paraphrase philosopher Jim Rohn, because it teaches us to behave in new ways.

People who take an active leadership role in their lives tend to be good thinkers; great leaders tend to be great thinkers.

MAKE TIME TO THINK

Too often, people confuse activity with accomplishment. As we all know, it's easy to be incredibly busy and still accomplish little. Author Amy Salzman observed that most people aren't too busy to look up from the grindstone—they're just afraid of what they might find when they do.

But taking the time to look up and think is a good thing. Thinking helps separate the mundane things in your life from the significant. It can help to clarify your direction and your purpose.

When I'm home in Denver, I usually devote fifteen to thirty minutes each afternoon to uninterrupted thought. I drive a couple of miles to the nearest Starbucks. I don't take my cell phone; I bring only a pad of paper and a pencil. I think about my business, the next speech I'm going to give, the arguments I want to present. Sometimes I think about ways I can be a better father, husband, or friend.

TAKE CONTROL OF YOUR LIFE

Many people feel paralyzed by their lack of control over life.

What can you do about it? For one thing, focus on all the things you *do* control. In doing so, you take control over your life and begin to lead your life, rather than letting life lead you.

For example, you can't control your looks—they are, for the most part, determined genetically. But you can control your appearance.

You can't control how much talent you have in a given area. But you can control how much effort you expend to develop the talent that you are born with.

You can't control your IQ. But you can control how well and how hard you think.

James, for example, barely got accepted to the university where he applied. As a high school student, he hadn't taken his studies or his future seriously. Early IQ testing had suggested that James was of only average intelligence.

But in college, James was inspired by a professor. He realized that while he couldn't change the genetic predisposition of his IQ, he could control how long and how well he studied. He took an optional course on study techniques and began to discipline himself to crack the books while his friends were out partying.

He graduated with a high grade point average that surpassed even his own expectations. Then a recruiter from a Fortune 100 company drew out the reason for James's academic success and realized the same responsibility and attitude would be an asset in his organization. Today James is on a fast track to high-level leadership.

MOTIVATION

Motivation refers to why we do what we do.

It's a question each of us must ask ourselves: In acting as a leader in life, how do we remain motivated? Another way to ask that question is to ask, *What gives my life meaning?*

In my conversations with business and community leaders over the years, they've talked frequently about how important it is to motivate others, to keep the fires of passion and commitment burning in their teammates and colleagues.

One of the quickest ways to burn out is to stop doing what you enjoy. The more successful you are, the greater the risk that you'll move into a position that will take you away from doing those things you're really good at doing and really like to do. You may assume greater responsibilities and as a result have less time to spend doing what you care most about.

How do we keep ourselves motivated? Here are a few of the techniques I have discovered over the years used by leaders, both titled and nontitled:

1. Make time to reflect

How much in business and life do we all miss out on because we don't take time to reflect on what is happening in our lives and what we can learn from these things?

2. Remember to dream

Some people are so caught up with day-to-day tasks that they forget to dream about the future. As a result, they don't aspire high enough, or far enough, for themselves or their organizations. Ask yourself: What do I dream of accomplishing in my life? In my career?

3. Mirror those who are successful around you

Find role models worthy of your attention, those who lead their lives and organizations in the manner in which you aspire to lead, who have made a difference to others as you would like to.

4. Retreat to advance

At least once a year (if not more often), set aside a day to review your life and objectives. You may want to remove yourself from the distractions of a typical day by "retreating" to a location where you are inaccessible by phone or e-mail.

5. Mentor someone else

One of the best ways to distill what you know is to share it with others. Moreover, helping another person grow can be a rewarding way to keep yourself motivated.

6. Enjoy the journey

It would be silly to say to yourself, "I'm going on vacation, but I have no intention of enjoying myself." Yet that is exactly what happens to us when we become too busy to take time to appreciate our journey in life. Take a moment to be grateful for what you have. Feeling grateful is one sure antidote to negativity.

7. Live like a *victor*, not a *victim*

When bad things happen to good people, we say they are "victims of circumstance." Yet it is easy to spend too much time feeling like a victim, rather than asking, "What am I going to do to make it better?"

The fact is, we can learn from difficult situations or languish in them. The decision is ours.

8. Search for the pony

An old favorite joke of mine illustrates the positive attitude of the person who takes responsibility for his or her life, even in those circumstances they don't completely control.

Twin boys were born to two happy parents. But as the children grew, the parents noticed a dramatic difference in the outlook each had on life.

One boy was completely negative. His perspective was consistently one of gloom and doom. No matter what happened, he was downhearted. He was able to find a rain cloud in the sunniest sky.

The other boy was buoyant and looked at everything positively. No matter what happened, he could find the silver lining in the darkest cloud.

The parents began to worry that each child had a problem. So one Christmas they attempted a bold experiment to try to change their sons' dispositions.

For the boy with the negative attitude, they bought the most wonderful gifts: a new bike, a train set, board games, and other fun diversions.

To the boy with the positive attitude, they gave a pile of horse manure.

On Christmas morning, the boy who was negative was led into a room containing all his wonderful gifts. But rather than being delighted, he complained, "The bike will become dirty and scratched the first time I ride it, and the other toys will break or wear out."

Their other son, upon seeing the pile of manure, shocked his parents by instantly shouting in glee.

"Why are you so excited?" they exclaimed.

He replied, "With all this manure, there's got to be a pony in here somewhere!"

My point? When something bad happens, the challenge is to search for the pony, not with the naive enthusiasm of the boy in the story but with the informed optimism of a leader.

REMEMBER THE SELF-MASTERY INDEX

I think of the "self-mastery index" as the ratio between promises made and promises kept—both to oneself and to others. If your mouth keeps making promises that you can't keep, there is a great deal of room for improvement. Integrity, after all, is measured by the distance between your lips and your life. If you want to be a leader in your own life and in the lives of others, you've got to follow through on your own promises, whether you have a title or not.

LEADERSHIP ACTION POINTS

STIMULATE YOUR BRAIN

Reading outside your area of expertise, or outside your comfort zone, can stimulate your thinking, whether that means picking up an interesting new book or thumbing through a new issue of a magazine.

A manager of an auto parts store I know was reading about how the hotel industry creates loyal customers, and he was struck by Doubletree Hotels' practice of providing guests with free chocolate-chip cookies at check-in. So he decided to try a similar idea in his business. When he delivered parts purchased from his store, he came bearing cold beverages for the mechanics. The idea was a huge hit and helped to earn him the loyalty of his customers.

Find ways to introduce yourself to new concepts and ideas. Just following the same familiar terrain will take you to the same familiar places and lead you to the same familiar conclusions. To reach a new or exotic destination requires taking a different route. Go outside your comfort zone: Occasionally read different publications or take a "field trip" to visit businesses you've never been to before.

Schedule a regular time for thinking. Pick a location conducive to thinking where you will not be distracted or interrupted. Schedule fifteen to thirty minutes to think (it is harder than it seems). Be sure to write down your insights.

RECORD YOUR INSIGHTS

Everyone has good ideas. Our problem isn't a lack of ideas but a lack of recall. Ideas are fleeting; they must be captured. I find that some of the biggest payoffs from thinking occur when I record my thoughts and review my notes later and add to or modify them. (The outline for this chapter was initially done on a piece of scrap paper in a restaurant in New York, and was revised and improved upon later.)

PICK A PROBLEM

Is there a problem that irritates you? Are there concerns in your workplace or community that you feel should be addressed?

When you see a problem worthy of your attention, ask, "How can I make a difference?" Assume you can make a difference, even if only a small one.

When it comes to problem solving in today's complex world, complete solutions are rare. Usually there isn't a single grand answer, but many answers that require the contributions of many different people or parties.

Remember, spotting a problem is easy. Anybody can do that. In fact, merely calling attention to a problem is called complaining. *Solving* a problem is harder; it requires an act of leadership. Most people would rather complain than contribute to a solution. Remember, more people regret things they wish they *had* done, rather than things they wish they hadn't. There is a long-term price for not following your heart.

THE POWER OF FOCUS

Energy and persistence conquer all things.
—BENJAMIN FRANKLIN

THE IMPORTANCE OF FOCUS

I have a friend named Bill who lives just outside of Kalamazoo, Michigan. Several years ago, he bought a new house on the edge of a lush wooded area. Bill likes to feed birds, so upon moving in, Bill put a feeder up in his backyard. But before the sun even set that evening, squirrels were swinging off the bird feeder and chasing the birds away. Bill realized that he had to do something or the birds would soon be too scared to come near the feeder, so for the next two weeks he declared war on the squirrels. Bill isn't a mean guy and wouldn't do anything to hurt the squirrels, but he was willing to use any peaceful means necessary to keep them out of his bird feeder.

He tried greasing the post the bird feeder was on, but that didn't work. Stumped, Bill visited his local hardware store and bought a "squirrel-proof bird feeder," an odd-looking feeder with wire mesh wrapped around it. The label said it was guaranteed, so Bill took it home and put it in his backyard.

But by sunset, squirrels were once again swinging off the

bird feeder. Bill was now really upset, and the next day he took the feeder back to the hardware store. He asked to see the manager, demanding a full refund.

"Calm down," the store manager told him. "I could have told you when you bought it that there is no such thing as a squirrel-proof bird feeder."

Bill looked at him in disbelief. You mean we can land a man on the moon and send instantaneous messages via satellite to anywhere around the world, but our best and brightest scientists and engineers can't design and manufacture a bird feeder that can outsmart an animal with a brain the size of a pea?

"Yep," said the retailer.

"Why not?" Bill persisted.

"Let me ask you something, sir," the man replied. "How much time on average have you spent in the last two weeks trying to keep the squirrels out of your bird feeder?" Bill thought it over for a moment and responded, "Maybe ten to fifteen minutes a day."

"And how much time do you think the squirrels spend each day trying to get in?"

The answer, Bill learned, is almost every waking squirrel moment; squirrels spend 98 percent of their waking hours looking for food. In fact, they are unique in the animal kingdom in that they would rather eat than procreate; they prefer foraging to fooling around. This just goes to show the kind of focus the squirrel brings to its mission.

The moral of this story: Focus and determination beat brains and intellect every time. You don't necessarily have to be smarter or better educated to succeed. Your power lies in your ability to focus on doing what is important. If you focus on the right things, and work at them often, you will achieve exceptional results.

THE DANGERS OF DRIFTING

One of the most important qualities of effective leadership is focus. Without focus, it is impossible to move forward to achieve your goals. Effective leaders, whatever their title, are able to keep themselves and those around them on task. Those who lack focus in their personal lives and in their careers tend to drift.

Years ago, on one of the first cruises my wife and I ever took, I visited the bridge of the behemoth ocean liner we were sailing on and spoke with the captain. I asked him about the biggest seas he had ever sailed in with that ship. He told me he had been in seas with ninety-foot waves.

Impressed, I inquired about how he had managed to keep the ship intact. He told me that while ninety-foot waves were daunting, the ship could negotiate them quite handily as long as it didn't lose power.

"If you lose power in big seas in any boat, you're in serious trouble. Under power," he explained, "the boat can stay perpendicular to the waves. Without power, the boat would drift parallel to the waves and be capsized or swamped."

That is the danger of drifting.

DRIFTING VS. WAITING

In acting as a leader, you can handle just about anything that comes your way as long as you don't lose power and drift. Power, in this sense, is the ability to stay engaged in what is going on. It doesn't mean that you have control over every situation, any more than a boat has control over the waves. Rather, it is the ability to engage the situation with intent, with *focus.*

Drifting and waiting are very different things.

Waiting is an intentional choice. It requires patience and deliberation.

Drifting takes away your power of choice.

When you wait, you believe that something will happen, although you may not know when. Instead of acting rashly or impetuously, you pause to gather information and seek insight.

Drifting results from rudderlessness and lack of direction. When you drift, it doesn't even take particularly large waves to capsize the boat.

It's all too easy to become distracted or lulled into complacency. Before you know it, you are drifting. A simple lack of attention can cause you to lose the power of purpose and engagement. Instead of initiating action, you become paralyzed. Rather than acting, you find yourself acted upon.

DISTRACTION IS DETRIMENTAL

According to the National Association of Professional Planners, the average American's desk has about fifty-two hours of unfinished work on it.

A recent study of knowledge workers found that they face a distraction every eleven minutes on average, and that once distracted, it takes them twenty-five minutes to get back to the task at hand.

According to a study conducted at the University of Michigan in 2005, 20 to 40 percent of a worker's productivity is eaten up by "task switching"—that is, the time it takes to mentally reengage when shifting from one task to another.

We live in a world of perpetual distraction. We are never "caught up," whatever that means. Multitasking, once valued as a productivity tool, now more often than not creates a sense of activity while actually decreasing output.

The unimportant and the trivial consume the time we should spend doing significant, meaningful work.

And it comes about because we neglect to focus.

Each of us faces demands beyond our control. Customers make requests, colleagues ask for assistance, and bosses—both enlightened and unenlightened—pile on the work. These are valid explanations for why it is hard to focus. But they are not an excuse for being unfocused.

The goal of anyone who wants to act as a leader is to move beyond the perpetual distractions we face and focus on what really matters.

During a recent convention, I was about to give a presentation to a group of executives in a North Denver hotel. On my way to the meeting room, I noticed several computer terminals in the lobby for hotel guests to use. Although I was scheduled to speak in fifteen minutes, I couldn't resist the opportunity to quickly log on and check my e-mail. The fact is there was nothing urgent in my in-box. The few e-mails I dispatched may have given me a sense of "keeping up," but checking them was a distraction from the real work I was doing. In our wired world, it's easy to become distracted or even addicted to cell phones, BlackBerrys, and the like. It reminded me of how diligently we have to work to stay focused.

ESTABLISH AN AGENDA

To stay focused, you need an agenda. Your a_____
hope to accomplish in both the short term an____
It means visualizing your final goal so that the ____
you closer to completion.

We often complain about the unplanned things in our day. They *can*, of course, present an incredible opportunity. For instance, by striving to increase ROI (Relationships, Outcomes, and Improvements), we may be able to spot new opportunities: a disgruntled customer, a discouraged coworker, a time- or money-saving idea, or a product improvement.

But to lead effectively, we can't wait for random events to help us achieve our goals. Our challenge is to plan to do things of significance and impact, then strategically pursue them.

I was conducting a seminar in Pittsburgh and, at the morning break, a man approached me. I had talked about how important it was to have a written long-range plan. He said, "Do you have a written long-range plan?" I said, "Yes, I do." He said, "Can I see it?" He wanted to see if I practiced what I preached. I said, "Well, I left it at home. I don't carry it with me when I'm on the road." He said, "You really should. Would you like to see my long-range goals?"

I had a feeling I didn't really have a choice. He reached into his wallet and took out an index card that had been cut down to size. On the index card were three goals. "Goal number one: Retire at age sixty-five, financially independent. Goal number two: Maintain excellent physical condition and health. Goal number three: Travel extensively throughout the United States broad." Three very simple goals on a worn and tattered index card that he kept in his wallet.

He then asked me, "How old do you think I am?" Now, admittedly, I am not a good judge of age, but he looked to be in his late forties or early fifties. He informed me he was two years away from retirement—he was sixty-three years of age. And I could tell just from looking at him that he was in excellent physical condition and health.

Then he went on to say, "You know, when I retire, I won't be outrageously wealthy, but I have enough money saved up that I don't have to depend on anyone to support me. If the Social Security system fails, I'll be okay." He had achieved financial independence.

He then told me that he had visited most of the fifty states and several foreign countries. After he retired, he planned to spend three to six months per year traveling abroad. He had obviously gone a long way in accomplishing the three life goals that he'd written on that index card.

He asked me, "Do you know how I've been able to accomplish all this? You can hear about an idea in a seminar. You can read about it in a book. But when you meet the idea in action, it has a certain impact on you." He said, "When I wake up each morning, I take out this card as I put together my daily to-do list. And I ask myself, 'Is what I'm doing today moving me closer to one of these three long-range goals?' If it isn't, I don't prioritize it, and very often I don't do it."

He learned that having a clear focus helped him evaluate what he was doing each day to determine if it would help him achieve the picture he held for his life, his future view. That is the power of focus.

David Campbell wrote a very clever book called *If You Don't Know Where You're Going, You'll Probably End Up Somewhere Else*. He's right. Your plan should include important goals. The picture we hold of our lives is the ultimate destination. The purpose is what propels us toward the destination. Priorities help.

Many people begin their workday by asking themselves what they need to get done. People who act as leaders ask a slightly different question: What important things do I plan to accomplish?

What "needs to be done" are often daily activities: phone calls returned, reports completed, and responses to e-mails. While necessary, they are often not very important in the bigger picture.

Contrast that to the important things to be accomplished: establishing long-range goals and taking steps toward meeting them; improving relationships with partners; increasing revenues; creating new projects.

PRIORITIZE

Understanding the relative importance of the things we do and spend time on is key to being efficient and effective.

Do you find that at the end of a typical day you've accomplished everything *except* the most important item on your list of "to do"s? That is an example of "reversed prioritization." The easy things get done and the important things stay undone. People who act successfully as leaders, whatever their title, learn to prioritize.

Creating a daily list of things to do is only part of the solution. Knowing what is most important on that list, and choosing to complete it first, is the other part.

LIVE INTENTIONALLY

You can't inject more time into your life. The challenge for all of us is to put more life into our time. In other words, making more progress, getting more results, and making greater contributions. That is what acting as a real leader is all about.

Most of the so-called defining moments of our lives really aren't. College graduation, marriage, and retirement are often called defining moments. In reality, they are commemorative moments. Graduation commemorates how you spent the past four years. Marriage commemorates the courtship leading up to it. Retirement commemorates a life at work. In each instance, the person has been defined long before the moment occurred.

What are the moments that define you? They are right now. Each moment we live helps to define us. People who act as leaders in their lives, and in the lives of others, understand this and choose to live *intentionally*.

By focusing attention and care on each moment, we can create a legacy of accomplishment and achievement at work and in life—in everything we do.

LEADERSHIP ACTION POINTS

ELIMINATE ACTIVITIES THAT DON'T ADD VALUE

None of us has more than twenty-four hours in each day. Your goal should be to spend as much of this precious resource as possible on the things that are important to you.

Have you attended a meeting in the past week that was a complete waste of time? If you find yourself in the midst of a meeting with no payoff to you or the other participants, excuse yourself to attend to a more pressing matter (and at that point, any matter qualifies). Better yet, work to avoid such meetings altogether.

The great advancements of history came about as a result of the ways individuals used their resources: their time and expertise, and the time and expertise of others.

How you manage those precious resources will determine how effective you are in life—whatever your title.

IDENTIFY YOUR MVP ACTIVITIES

In sports, "MVP" stands for Most Valuable Player. For leaders, I use MVP differently. When applied to leadership, MVP activities are those that are *M*ost *V*aluable and *P*rofitable.

If you're like me, you do fifty, seventy-five, or a hundred different things every day. The dilemma is that only a few of those activities really count for much.

What six to eight MVP activities give you the biggest payback on your investment of time and energy? Develop a list of your MVP activities. . . .

Now work to spend 60 to 80 percent of each day doing them. You still have 20 to 40 percent of each day to deal with interruptions, requests, putting out fires, and emergencies that you couldn't plan for.

POWER WITH PEOPLE

Leadership is the art of getting extraordinary performance
from ordinary people.
—ANONYMOUS

PEOPLE MAKE IT HAPPEN

Everything we accomplish happens not just because of our efforts but through the *efforts of others*.

A CFO, discussing the leadership potential of a mutual acquaintance, said to me, "I know he is very productive, maybe the most productive person I know. What I haven't seen yet is his ability to leverage his efforts and get results through others. That is what will determine how successful he will be as a leader."

To accomplish any significant goal requires the support and cooperation of others. The biggest difference between people who *manage* others, versus people who *lead* others, is how they develop those under them: This is true whether they manage or lead their families, a fund-raising effort, a project team, or a company.

Power with People

In my first job out of college, I was an account executive. My assistant was a very competent woman named Teri. We had a good working relationship.

The first time I hosted a client visit at that company, I gave the client a tour of the printing facilities and was introducing him to the people he interacted with by phone, to give him a chance to put faces with names.

We stopped by Teri's cubicle. Being new and somewhat naive, I introduced her by saying, "This is Teri. She works for me."

I'll never forget how Teri reacted.

"I work with you, Mark, not for you," she calmly responded.

I learned an important leadership lesson that day. Of course, I wish Teri had waited for the client to leave before giving me that lesson. But although the timing wasn't ideal, the lesson was profound. Teri was right. My choice of words portrayed a misconception about having power over someone because of my position. As all leaders know, untitled or not, leadership is power *with* people, not power *over* people.

Leaders vs. Managers

Managers have employees.	Leaders win followers.
Managers react to change.	Leaders create change.
Managers have good ideas.	Leaders implement them.
Managers communicate.	Leaders persuade.

Managers direct groups.	Leaders create teams.
Managers try to be heroes.	Leaders make heroes of everyone around them.
Managers take credit.	Leaders take responsibility.
Managers exercise power *over* people.	Leaders exercise power *with* people.

Your Impact on Others

Do you build people up or tear them down?

Encourage or discourage others?

Try to be the hero, or make heroes out of those around you?

I've found that those who aspire to lead (or lead better) learn to build people up, encourage them, and make them into heroes.

According to researcher Tom Rath at Gallup, the number-one reason why people quit their jobs is lack of appreciation. Everyone wants to feel significant, to be recognized for what they do. As nineteenth-century British prime minister Benjamin Disraeli said, "The greatest good you can do for another is not just to share your riches but to reveal to him his own."

Let me give you an example of that in the person of Sam Preston, who retired from S. C. Johnson Wax after many years of service as an executive vice president. While he was at Johnson Wax, Sam used to make it a point to send handwritten notes when he noticed somebody doing something that merited recognition. The note would say, "Congratulations on a job well done," with the letters "DWD" scrawled across the top. DWD stood for "damned well done." When he retired, the company held a retirement party for him. He was amazed at the number of people who lined up clutching wrinkled yellow pieces of paper, fifteen years old, with "DWD" scrawled across the top. That little act of recognition and appreciation meant so much to the people under him that they kept those notes all those years. An insignificant act with a significant outcome. The lesson: It's important to make people feel appreciated. It's even more important to let people know that there is someone who believes in them so much that he or she will not let them be less than they can be.

Character, Competence, Connection

To harness the power of others, you have to persuade them to follow your lead. This is even more important for untitled leaders who don't have the authority to promote or fire. To get others to follow you requires character, competence, connection—what I call the 3 Cs.

CHARACTER

Those who wish to influence others understand how important character is, whatever their title. We all have blind spots. To see through our blind spots, we need to be open enough to seek input from others. To get that honest input, we must earn their trust.

The word *hypocrite* comes from a Greek word literally meaning "actor." Greek actors put on masks and assumed to be what they weren't. While that ability is important for thespians, it is a terrible quality in a leader. Trust is vital to leadership. If others can't trust you, how can they follow you?

Management guru Tom Peters when asked, "How do I get people to trust me?" answered: "Be trustworthy." What does that mean?

If you don't know something, say so.
Don't make promises you can't keep.
Underpromise and overdeliver.
Be careful to create realistic expectations.

Another essential aspect of character is humility—a focus on others born out of concern for them. As Rick Warren, author of *The Purpose-Driven Life,* says, "Humility isn't thinking less of yourself. It is thinking of your self *less.*" The opposite of humility isn't pride; it is self-absorption. Few people can lead or inspire others, at work or at home, when they are self-absorbed.

COMPETENCE

There are few pleasures I enjoy more in life than a good shoe shine. While changing planes in Detroit recently, I decided to get my shoes shined. But before deciding whether or not to give the shoe-shine guy near my gate my business, I watched him for a few minutes to determine the quality of his work. The shoes he shined looked terrific, so I decided to give him a try.

As he worked, I commented on the quality of the shoe shines I had gotten in other airports, mentioning how difficult it was to gauge the kind of shoe shine I would get in places I hadn't been in before. He looked up at me with astonishment. "It's easy to tell if you're going to get a good shine," he told me.

"Just look at the shoes of the guy giving the shine. If they ain't fine, walk on by." I glanced at his shoes; they literally shone. They were a walking billboard proclaiming his competence.

People who act as leaders exude competence—by their actions, by their appearance, and in everything they undertake.

CONNECTION

When we act effectively as leaders, those around us bond with us—not because of our position or title in the organization, but because of their relationship with us. But that kind of emotional connection can only occur when you are genuinely concerned about others. You can't achieve that connection through gimmicks, tricks, or shortcuts. When you care for others—even those you have only limited personal contact with—it shows. Being nice to others is fundamental.

In their insightful *Harvard Business Review* article "Competent Jerks, Lovable Fools and the Formation of Social Networks," Tiziana Casciaro and Miguel Sousa Lobo reported that when people need help getting a job done, they'll choose a congenial colleague over a more capable one. Of course, it is important to be competent. But if you want to be the person others turn to for help, it helps to be likable, as well. We like people who are similar to us, people we are familiar with, people who have reciprocal feelings about us, and people who are considerate, cheerful, generous.

Motivating Others

People do things for *their own* reasons, not for *yours*. To be an effective leader, you need to know how to motivate others.

The fact is, people need reasons to do things. There are overwhelming demands on everyone's time and energy. To enlist the support and service of others, you need to show them how they will benefit.

Many years ago, in a midwestern city, I tested a new seminar titled How to Motivate People. The majority of the 300 or so members of the audience were managers, although a significant number lacked executive titles. Those folks were particularly interested in how to motivate others, especially those people who didn't report to them and over whom they had no power.

As I was discussing the various carrots and sticks that could be used to motivate others, I asked them, "How many of you have ever been asked by an employer or boss what motivates *you*?" After a brief pause, a few hands went up—by my quick estimate, no more than 15 percent of the group.

Since then, I've gotten similar responses from other audiences over the years. My point? Most attempts to motivate others are based on assumptions. Managers *think* they know what motivates another person. But they rarely do the work of finding out if their assumptions are true. So ask others what motivates them! One of the most effective means of engaging others is to simply tell them, "I need your help." Your very request *invites* participation (instead of commanding it). You also make clear that the other person's opinion matters.

Not all people will live up to your expectations. But while you may not get all that you hoped or expected, you will always get more than you would have gotten otherwise. One of the greatest compliments you can be paid as a leader is to have someone say that you helped them be better than they thought they could be.

Confronting Problems

Few people like confrontation. And nobody likes to be confronted.

But of course in leading others, confrontation is necessary at times. If you avoid confrontation when it is needed, eventually others won't take you seriously.

The solution? To confront *problems*, not *people*.

It is never wise to ignore conflict in an attempt to smooth things over in a relationship. Doing so results in the opposite over the long haul, and it can cause resentment among colleagues and employees.

When you need to confront others, show concern for the other person as you address the problem. Remember, most problems require the other person's cooperation to resolve. Alienating the other person will almost always doom the process.

Focus on correcting the other person's behavior or actions rather than judging the person. Be willing to examine the role your behavior and actions play in the relationship. Talking about "what" went wrong, rather than "who" went wrong, will make those around you much less defensive.

Don't Be Afraid to Challenge Those Around You

A popular university professor, addressing a large crowd of students who showed up for the first day of his course, began by telling them how hard the course would be and how much extra work would be required. A few got up and left.

He then told the students that the effort required for a passing grade would be what it took to get an A in most other classes. A few more picked up their books and departed.

He admonished those who remained that it wasn't enough to be interested in the course. To succeed, students needed to be passionate about the subject. And with that, several more bewildered students vacated the room.

To the much smaller but obviously determined group of students left, the professor finally said, "Don't worry. The course won't be nearly as hard as I've described it. I just wanted to make sure that I had the most committed students in this course."

Rather than sugarcoat the work they would have to do, his approach was to challenge his students so that only the most committed would stay on. It can be an effective tool for anyone who acts as a leader.

When you undersell what you need from others out of fear of rejection, you tend to get little in return. Ask for a big commitment and you'll increase the likelihood of getting a big effort back.

Set an Example

As a leader, titled or not, your job is to act as a thermostat, not as a thermometer. Show others the attitude, commitment, and performance you expect from them. Industrialist Harvey Firestone said, "You get the best out of others when you give the best of yourself." That is true for parents, teachers, managers, and business owners.

Getting the best out of others—and helping others give their best—is the very definition of people power.

LEADERSHIP ACTION POINTS

EXPRESS YOUR APPRECIATION

To act like a leader, celebrate the success of those around and under you as if it were your own. Express your appreciation regularly.

ASK OTHERS WHAT MOTIVATES THEM

Here are some of the questions you can ask others to help you determine what motivates them.

What do you like about work the most? What is your favorite activity?

What do you like to do the least?

What is your typical work style?

Whom do you enjoy working with? Whom do you dislike working with, and why?

What annoys you about being part of a team?

What do you enjoy about teamwork?

What do you hope to be doing in ten years?

What values do you try to live your life by?

COLLABORATE

When it comes to decision making, the oft-used acronym TEAM is true: Together Everyone Accomplishes More. On projects, find ways to collaborate with other people.

That way, each individual's insights become learning points for the rest of the group.

To engage others, ask:

- What do you think we should do?
- What would you do if you were in my shoes?
- What opportunities are we missing?
- What information or ideas do you have that would be beneficial?

PRACTICE DIPLOMATIC CONFRONTATION

Think of a teammate or colleague who is causing a problem. Rather than confronting the person, consider what behavior of his or hers needs to change. Once you've identified the behavior(s), reassure the person of your regard for him or her, but address the needed behavior change.

THE POWER OF PERSUASIVE COMMUNICATION

We have too many high sounding words, and too few actions
that correspond with them.

—Abigail Adams

COMMUNICATING IS NOT THE OBJECTIVE

A sales manager approached me after I had finished speaking about leadership at his association's meeting. His mood seemed somewhere between perplexed and provoked.

"You talked about how leaders need to communicate persuasively," he complained. "But I have a problem with the word 'communication.' It's far too ambiguous. I told my team I wasn't interested in communication; their job is *understanding*! If the sale isn't made, there was no understanding."

That sales manager was right. Communicating *isn't* the objective in business or life. The objective is understanding. Communication is simply the tool to accomplish that.

It reminds me of the night our family went out to dinner. As we waited for our table, my wife Darla was reading the specials board out loud. "Look, boys, 'All You Can Eat Fish.'" At that point, Jack, five at the time, responded with exasperation. "Oh no!" he said. "All you can eat is fish?! I wanted a hamburger!"

In one study, poor communication was cited as the cause of poor employee performance 80 percent of the time (if you define communication broadly enough, you could say it is responsible for 100 percent of the problems we face).

Communicating *effectively* is what acting as a leader is all about, whatever your position or title.

A Subtle Change Can Make a Dramatic Difference

My friend Jerry was asked to eulogize the life of a departed friend. Jerry prepared his remarks carefully. Just before the service, the man's wife begged him, "Jerry, I don't want this to be sad and depressing."

So what did Jerry do? He changed one word to three words in his prepared remarks. The rest of his comments he delivered exactly as he had written them.

What three words did he change?

He changed the word "funeral" to the phrase "celebration of life."

Words have the extraordinary power to change our thinking, our emotions, to affect our attitudes and alter results. People who act as leaders in their life, like Jerry, understand what a big difference even a few small words can make in reaching out to others.

From Telling to Selling

The belief that an idea, plan, project, or solution is so good that it doesn't have to be sold is foolish. The best idea in the world won't do anyone any good if no one accepts it. You have to be able to convince others of the advantages or strengths of your ideas.

Yet some people feel selling is beneath them. I think the reason is that people confuse selling with manipulation. They assume a salesperson is just out to meet his or her goal or agenda at their expense. Somehow the entire process has become tainted by a few unscrupulous individuals.

Selling is simply helping people make a decision that is good for them.

When you have a good idea, product, service, or solution that can benefit others, it is your *responsibility* to sell it. Telling others about it isn't enough.

The One Sure Way to Establish Rapport

Rapport refers to "a feeling of comfortableness." We tend to like people who we think are like us.

Selling involves the critical importance of establishing rapport. One effective technique is to look for similarities with the other person. Do you enjoy the same activities? Have friends in common?

But there is a much easier and natural way to establish rapport. Ask yourself, What is the one thing I always have in common with another person or group of people?

The answer: *Their best interest.*

When people know you are interested in their best interests, and in helping them meet their needs, they will trust you. It's human nature. And that genuine interest in helping others and making a positive difference is the essence of leadership.

Influence

People who act as leaders care less about the impressions they make than the influence they exert on others to take positive action. Effective leaders know what they want to accomplish with every conversation they have, every e-mail, phone call, or speech.

When they communicate, they "begin with the end in mind." Ask yourself, What do I want the person I'm communicating with to think, feel, and do when I'm done?

FEED BACK AND FEED FORWARD

One of the corniest stories I know is about a man driving up a mountain road in a Jeep. Coming down the mountain in the other lane is a woman in a Jeep. As she passes, she leans out and yells, "Pig!"

The man is offended! Why is that woman calling him a name and making a judgment on his character?

As he looks back in his rearview mirror at the woman behind him, he smashes into a hog that is standing in the middle of the road.

The woman wasn't criticizing him, but rather warning him of what lay ahead. Unfortunately, her feedback was limited by time. Had circumstances allowed, she might have said,

"There is a large farm animal ahead in the middle of the road—be careful!"

Such are the pitfalls of communication. When you don't take time to communicate clearly, the potential for misunderstanding—and even disaster—is high.

One way to make sure another person has heard and understood what you've said is to ask them to repeat it back to you in their own words. You might say, "I want to make sure I've explained that clearly. Would you tell me how you understand what I've said?"

Getting feedback is an excellent way to adjust your message and ensure understanding. The one drawback is that it is "after the fact." To increase the odds of future success, why not *feed forward*—provide people with the information they need to be successful before they undertake something.

Feedback evaluates what has been done.

Feed forward clarifies expectations of what needs to be accomplished.

Feedback is *remedial.*

Feed forward is *preventative.* Rather than waiting until later to determine if you've communicated clearly, it gives people the answers in advance to prevent possible problems from arising.

TELL A BETTER STORY

Whenever I meet a person who has heard me speak, I like to ask them what they remember about what I said. No one says to me, "I love the insights you gave us about customer loyalty" or "Your point about taking responsibility seemed so dead on." Instead they say, "I remember that story you told about Fred, your postal carrier" or "I loved the story about the squirrels and the bird feeder."

PEOPLE REMEMBER STORIES

Stories are the coat pegs of the mind. They are where people hang their ideas. Once they have a memorable story to help them remember, they can recall whatever important moral or point you have to make.

People who act as leaders know that stories illustrate and facts validate. Facts and statistics support—but never substitute for—a good narrative.

Good stories are powerful because they include an emotional component. They communicate not only what happened but how the person feels about what happened. Statistics may allow us to draw conclusions, but they seldom motivate us to make commitments.

There is an old poem that says, "I'd rather see a sermon than hear one any day. I'd rather one would walk with me than simply point the way."

Telling an entertaining story is important, but *being* the story is better. Reinforcing who you are through the stories you tell helps to create credibility with your audience.

Everything You Do Makes a Difference

In the mornings when I'm not traveling, I drive my son Hunter to school.

One week while I was out of town for a trip, my wife Darla

drove Hunter. Traffic was light that particular morning, which prompted Hunter to ask his mom, "Where are all the damn drivers today?"

Darla was shocked by his language. "Why would you say that, honey?"

"Well," my son replied, "when Dad drives me to school the streets are full of damn drivers!"

Which goes to show you: Everything you do has an impact. Your actions either help improve others or diminish them. Others observe your behavior and are influenced by it, either for better or for worse.

Strive to live by a higher standard, knowing that you lead as much with actions as with words.

Call for Action

Too many communicate without a clear call to action. Every e-mail, phone call, voice mail, conversation, or speech should conclude with a request for action, with a "Let's do it." Let's move forward, take the next step, get involved, play our part, et cetera.

Jeff Salzman, a cofounder with Jimmy Calano of the training company CareerTrack, concludes his negotiations by asking, "Do I have your word on that?" It's a good technique to ensure commitment from others. Most people take the act of giving their word very seriously. If they are hesitant or reluctant, it will come to the surface at that point.

How Leaders Communicate

Others tell. *Leaders sell.*
Others impress. *Leaders influence.*

Others try to be heard. *Leaders strive to be understood.*
Others explain. *Leaders energize.*
Others inform. *Leaders inspire.*
Others relay only facts. *Leaders tell stories.*

The Power of Clarity

The Gettysburg Address is one of the greatest speeches in American history. Delivered by Abraham Lincoln at the scene of one of the Civil War's most costly battles, it contains only ten sentences. But in those few sentences, Lincoln was able to convey great truths in a powerful and unforgettable way.

What you may not know is that there was another speaker on the dais that day in Gettysburg—a senator named Edward Everett. Considered the most skilled orator of his time, Senator Everett traveled around the country addressing audiences. He was the equivalent of today's professional speaker. But while eloquent, he was also long-winded. His speech at Gettysburg lasted nearly two hours. Lincoln's short speech completely trumped Everett's endless oration.

Great leaders are not evaluated on the length at which they speak, but on the impact of their message.

What are your ten sentences as a leader?

LEADERSHIP ACTION POINTS

FOCUS ON THE OTHER PERSON

One of the biggest obstacles to effective communication is discounting another's point of view. Consciously or unconsciously, as most people listen, they ask themselves, "What does this mean to *me*?" Effective leaders help their audience answer that question by making it easy for them to grasp the message's impact.

SIMPLIFY THE MESSAGE

Several years ago, I attended a one-day leadership symposium for a telecommunications company. Using PowerPoint slides, upper management shared 138 "leadership imperatives" with those assembled. Now, I don't know about you, but I have a hard time remembering seven-digit phone numbers, much less 138 imperatives.

People who act effectively as leaders boil down the details. They make the world easy for others to understand.

The only thing people have less of today than disposable income is time. Effective leaders harness the power of the sound bite in an effort to make concepts easy to understand and repeat.

ENTERTAIN TO ENGAGE

To paraphrase Voltaire, the one unforgivable sin of communication is to be boring.

To make yourself heard and understood, you must find a way to grab your audience's attention.

It's something I first learned as a teenager from State Senator David Johnson, who told me, "Always remember, whether you're giving a sermon, teaching a class, or giving a speech, people want to be entertained."

You can't bore people into action. So try entertaining them instead.

THE POWER OF EXECUTION

Execution is the chariot of genius.
—WILLIAM BLAKE

WALKING THE WALK

Texans describe posers as "Big hat, no cattle." As Henry Ford famously said, "You cannot build a reputation on what you are going to do."

LEADERS HAVE HIGH IQS

If there is one irrefutable test of a leader, it is the results he or she produces. Successful leaders virtually always have a high IQ. I don't mean Intelligence Quotient, as measured by the Stanford-Binet test. I'm referring to what I call your *Implementation Quotient.* Having good ideas isn't enough—you have to be able to implement them.

Debbie aspired to be a sales leader. She understood the importance of professional development and was determined to study the best books and tapes available on selling. She'd spend one to two hours each day studying. Although she felt good about her disciplined approach to education, she was puzzled at her lack of sales results. Her problem? She didn't spend the balance of her day *implementing* what she'd learned. She did what was most *pleasant*—reading the material—not what was most *profitable*.

Intent without action is daydreaming. People who act as leaders couple their beliefs to their behavior. They get results.

Peter Schutz, a former CEO of Porsche, once told an audience I was a part of, "A bad decision well implemented is better than a brilliant decision not well implemented."

A Teacher with a High IQ

Sheila is an art teacher at a community rec center in Highlands Ranch, Colorado. Her class on clay sculpting is scheduled for an hour, but she regularly lets her students stay an extra half hour for which she isn't reimbursed.

If leadership is positive influence, then Sheila is a leader in capital letters. She is an incredible encourager of both students and their parents. Her class is about teaching children how to sculpt and glaze things out of clay. But she might begin a typical class by having the kids play Native American drums, followed by a story that teaches an important life lesson drawn from the early culture of the American West.

During the class, Sheila seizes all opportunities to teach, and not just about art. She'll explain the importance of working together, and tell her students that each child is unique and it is OK to be different.

Her power to positively influence is built on the careful attention she pays to each student's abilities and her willingness to work with each individually. She brings her own books, videos, and magazines to assist students in their particular projects and develop their specific talents.

When the parents arrive to pick up their kids, she discusses the child's progress. She noticed one little boy had problems with his spatial abilities, a challenge her own son had dealt with. After discussing it with his parents, she gave them a physician referral.

Another little boy created an Eskimo scene from his clay. Sheila cut a strip from a fur coat she had at home and brought it to class for the student so he could make blankets for his project.

I know what a wonderful leader Sheila is personally, because my sons Jack and Hunter are in her class. And thanks to her, both are excited about art, and Hunter has blankets in his Eskimo diorama.

Visioning

I've coined a term to describe what people who act successfully as leaders do: I call it *visioning*. *Vision* is a noun. *Visioning* is a verb, describing one's ability to articulate and achieve a vision.

For years, organizations have been enamored with the concept of having a "vision." "Visionary leaders" are those who see the grand view of the future and are able to articulate that vision eloquently to inspire those below them.

To me, the difference between vision and visioning is similar to the difference between creativity and innovation. Most people are pretty creative. Let me give you a case in point: How many times have you seen an advertisement or been shopping and noticed a new product that you had an idea for years earlier? How often have you said to yourself, "Hey, I thought of that!"

In other words, you *are* creative; we all have the ability to come up with new ideas.

Innovation, on the other hand, is the ability to implement those ideas. The man, woman, or company who took the same idea you had, then designed, manufactured, and distributed a resulting product, was *innovative*.

The Barriers to Execution

These are some of the things that hold people back from taking bold action and from implementing their ideas.

Paralysis by Analysis

At times, we analyze a problem to death rather than acting upon it. Yes, taking action without the proper consideration is risky, even dangerous. But an equal risk arises when you overstudy a situation rather than doing something about it.

If you are unsure whether or not you have all the information you need, ask yourself, Is additional information going to improve the quality or timeliness of taking action?

One manager I know encourages "little *l*" leadership. He says to employees, "If a customer has a problem, concern, or complaint, deal with it on the spot. Don't make it worse by trying to find me to determine what to do. After you've satisfied the customer, let me know what you did. If I can think of a way to do it better the next time, I'll coach you. In any event, you'll never get in trouble for taking the initiative to solve problems."

FEAR OF FAILURE

It is true that when you act, you may fail. It is also true that if you don't act, you'll never fail—but of course, you'll never achieve anything worthwhile, either.

No matter how much information you collect, success is never a sure thing. The fact is, people who act as leaders fail more often than others do. Why? Because they try more things and take more risks. Failure in the pursuit of a worthy cause is the price leaders pay for ultimate success.

CONFUSING TALKING WITH TAKING ACTION

Discussing a problem or opportunity is not part of implementing it. It doesn't increase your IQ. Discussion is a *precursor* to action.

At the end of each meeting or conversation, determine who is going to do what. Make sure everyone else has accepted responsibility for their specific tasks. Set a schedule for when these actions will occur. Identify a date and time to report back or reconvene on results.

ACCEPTING EXPLANATIONS AS EXCUSES

When something doesn't happen, there is always an explanation. But never accept an explanation as an excuse. "I didn't get the information I needed" or "The package arrived late" are all reasonable explanations, but they don't relieve the other person of responsibility. Excuses are like a free pass or a get-out-of-jail card. It is crippling to an individual or organization when explanations serve as excuses.

Instead, use explanations to figure out what happened, then look for the lesson that will prevent that something from happening again.

How to Increase Your IQ

Implementing an action is both an attitude and a skill. I believe the ideas below will go a long way toward increasing anyone's Implementation Quotient:

1. DREAM BIG

Decide what you want to accomplish. Think through what you will need to achieve your most ambitious goal: the resources of time, expertise, and the support of others.

Francis Ford Coppola said, "Work on nothing less than epic scale." Ask yourself, If we can turn the dream into reality, what will that look like?

2. PLAN SMALL

Big plans can be derailed by tiny details. Break big tasks into smaller "to do"s. A great way to create momentum is by completing as many little things as quickly as possible. You will begin to see noticeable progress toward your ultimate goal.

To create an effective plan, ask:

What needs to be done?
Why are we doing this?

Who is responsible for each task?
When will things happen?

Fill those four buckets with the necessary details to create a comprehensive and practical plan.

3. TEAM UP

This is where your people power skills are tested. Inspiring others around you to make positive change requires persuasive communication and people skills.

Whom do you need on your team? What role will each person play? Select those you need on the basis of skills and abilities, not personal preferences.

If it becomes impossible to achieve your "optimum outcome," what acceptable alternatives, if any, are you willing to settle for?

Hold others accountable for results rather than activity. People can look busy and accomplish little—measure what you treasure.

4. KEEP STRIVING

There are nights I go out and play a piece *perfectly*. Then, the next night, I go out and play it *better*.

—JEAN-PIERRE RAMPAL, flautist

Organizations are often on a crusade to find the best practices in their field or industry. They seek out the best techniques and ideas in the marketplace and implement them.

Individuals do that, as well. The problem, however, is that once a "best practice" has been adopted, most people and organizations breathe a collective sigh of relief and get back to business as usual. They quit looking for more best practices.

My suggestion is to toss out the notion of best practices. Do the best at whatever you're already doing—but always keep searching for *better practices*. Today's best practice is next year's discarded fad.

5. Act boldly

One thing the Marine Corps teaches is that it's better to be doing something than doing nothing. If you stay where you are, you're in the position where your enemy wants you to be. If you start doing something, you are changing the rules of the game.

—General Peter Pace, U.S. Marine Corps

Once you've got a plan and the resources you need, it's time to take decisive action. Remember, how you act will greatly influence the enthusiasm and commitment of those around you.

Don't just act once; keep on taking action until you succeed.

When you do, you'll find that you will achieve the kind of sustained results that most people only dream of attaining.

Facing Your Fears

Don't let fear prevent you from taking decisive action.

While I was in Australia on a speaking tour, I ran across an unusual opportunity: to bungee jump off a 150-foot bridge.

I consulted with people who had done it, as well as the people who ran the bungee-jump operation and who had orchestrated more than 40,000 jumps without death or serious injury. I spoke to a physician who assured me that bungee jumping was safe. So I decided to make the jump. I committed to it.

At the jump site, they had specially constructed a bridge that stood 150 feet high over a small pond of water. And as I started to climb the stairs to the top of that bridge, I discovered that the intellectual commitment to jump diminishes proportionate to one's height in the air.

The higher I climbed, the more I began to question my judgment and my common sense. By the time I made it to the top of the bridge, pure, unadulterated terror had set in. The pond below looked like a mud puddle. The people looked like ants. Cannes, a town twenty-two miles off in the distance, looked much closer to me than the water below.

And as I stood at the top of the bridge, I remembered reading about a part of the brain that takes over when we're afraid, a primitive part of the brain that we don't typically tap into in our daily lives. And I remember thinking that if I were going to go through with the jump, I would have to depend on that primitive part of the brain, because my logical, rational brain was telling me to get the heck out of there. I told the people who were helping to tie me up quickly so that I could get the jump over with, because I realized that I was very close to reneging on my decision to jump.

They wrapped the nylon climbing cord around my ankles several times, tied it to the end of the bungee cord, and had me stand on the edge of the bridge, looking at the 150-foot plunge below.

The bungee-cord operators said they were going to count backward from five. "When we get to one, we want you to leap out toward the ocean," they instructed. So they counted down to one—five, four, three, two, one—when, using that primitive part of my brain, I leapt out into space.

And I made an incredible discovery. Jumping is not at all scary. The only scary part is *thinking* about jumping. I plummeted down 150 feet, when, at the bottom, the bungee cord rebounded me back up almost 125 feet. It was the closest thing to flying I'd ever experienced. I felt weightless. After I had yo-yoed three or four times, I finally settled at the end of the cord, was lowered down to a raft, untied, and that was the end of my bungee jump.

This experience reminded me that most of the things we fear in our lives are not nearly as scary as we imagine when we finally confront them. I think that true leaders, once they have gathered their information and made a decision about a certain action, rely on the primitive part of the brain that propels them forward, without further thought, discussion, intellectualization, or rationalization. Once they've made a commitment to an action, they follow through with it, despite their trepidation or fear.

But there's another lesson that I learned from bungee-cord jumping. The woman who jumped after me had a more difficult time getting off the bridge. The bungee operators counted backward from five, eight or ten times. It took ten minutes to get her to jump. And when she finally did, she didn't jump so much as she fell. But when they finally had lowered her down to the raft and brought her into shore, I asked her, "What was it that finally made you jump off the bridge?" She said they only asked her two questions. Number one: How will you feel after you've jumped? And number two: How will you feel if you don't?

Next time you find yourself facing an important decision and you're not sure what to do, ask yourself two simple questions: When you've successfully confronted the challenge, how will you feel? And if you decide not to take that challenge, how will you feel, months and years later, about not having made that leap?

LEADERSHIP ACTION POINTS

DON'T LET RESISTANCE STOP YOU

Whenever you seek to make changes, you will encounter resistance, whether from a spouse, employees, committee members, or coworkers. There is always a headwind facing those who move confidently forward.

While it is important to listen to what others have to say, at times you simply have to make a decision and move forward despite their objections. It is rare that everyone will share your enthusiasm. Some will resist or complain. But the success of your efforts will bring them around. And if you're wrong, you'll know to change course.

ACT BOLDLY

In what ways are you acting tentatively in your efforts to positively affect others? Is there a behavior or two that would be more effective if you acted more boldly? You don't want to come across as cocky or arrogant. But leaders who know what they stand for and what is important to them act with confidence.

What areas of your life can you infuse with boldness?

THE POWER OF GIVING

If you truly desire happiness, seek and learn how to serve.
—ALBERT SCHWEITZER

WHY CHARLIE GAVE UP ON GIVING

Charlie "Tremendous" Jones is one of the most philanthropic people I know. Throughout his life, he has given lavishly of his time and money. So you can imagine my surprise when he announced to me and his other friends, "I've given up on giving."

There had to be more to the story, we knew.

He went on to explain: "Everything I have—my life, my potential, my time—was given to me. I've decided to spend the rest of my life *returning*."

Charlie wasn't talking about putting back into the world what he took out of it. He was talking about making the world a *better* place, which is what great leaders do.

Why do people give of themselves? They do so because:

1. Giving teaches us to look beyond ourselves.

It breaks down our preoccupation with "self," our absorption with how do "I" look and how do others perceive me. It reminds us that we are part of a larger community and that our navel is not the center of the universe.

2. Giving teaches us to be of greater service in helping others.

Giving is an art. That requires practice. After all, what is the point of having physical and emotional reserves if you don't share them?

3. Giving makes the world a better place.

Capitalism can be a great force for good. Having a generous spirit is an even stronger source for good. Together they make a powerful combination.

4. Giving makes us feel good.

We don't do good because we feel good.
We feel good because we do good.

It's Never Too Late

What does a retired farmer living in a retirement community and an elderly woman who always wanted a ride in a Rolls Royce have in common? Both have had their dreams come true thanks to the efforts of a man named Bob Haverstick.

The retired farmer yearned for one more chance to drive a tractor. So Bob located a nearby farm where the elderly farmer could be taken to make his dream come true.

And he arranged for the elderly woman to tour the city of Indianapolis in the style she always dreamed of, in a Rolls rented by Bob's organization.

Bob Haverstick left a senior position with a large corporation to dedicate his life to helping older men and women make their dreams come true. He found a way to help older people living in nursing homes, assisted-living facilities, hospice programs, and adult-care facilities by forming the nonprofit organization Never Too Late.

Thanks to Bob's vision and the help of financial supporters and volunteers, within five years of its inception, Never Too Late was able to grant fifteen to twenty wishes each month.

Here's what Bob says about Never Too Late: "Mostly, it is about making connections, networking in the best sense of the word, making people feel good about themselves. This program is about taking people who feel invisible and forgotten and showing them we care just because they are alive and with us. It is not about what they bring to the table or what they can do for us—it is about our remembering them and honoring them for all they have ever done or been all of their long lives."

WHAT CAN YOU GIVE?

People who want to make a positive difference in the world around them often wish to give of their time, expertise, money, and/or skills.

What made Bob's vision a reality was his willingness to give of himself. He left a secure corporate position to found Never Too Late, relying on only his time and talent. But he soon attracted others who wanted to offer their time, talent, and financial help.

Nonetheless, giving, for many people, is harder than it first appears. *USA Today* recently published a poll that asked people to finish the line "I'd give more, but . . ." The results?

- 84 percent said they doubted their donation would be put to good use.
- 80 percent said job demands left them no time to participate.
- 79 percent said they had no excess income to give.
- 70 percent said family commitments consumed their extra time.

From the responses above, do you recognize your own reason to give less of yourself than you'd like?

Remember, there are many ways to give. One easy way to give is to donate money. It's not hard to identify worthwhile charities and nonprofits that do an efficient job of putting the funds they receive to good use. If you're concerned that a donation won't be used properly, consider getting personally involved in the organization you're donating money to, as a way of tracking its use. Or fund your own project. Enlist your employer as a sponsor. Many organizations match dollars, and some make time available for community service.

If you don't have extra money to give, you can give of your time, expertise, or skills.

TO LEAD IS TO SERVE

Robert Greenleaf, in his book *Servant Leadership,* writes that he believes the whole purpose of leadership is to serve. He wrote his book at a time when leadership was often seen simply as a symbol of success and status. Greenleaf sounded a cautionary note, claiming that true leadership wasn't about what you achieved but what you gave. His book changed the way many think about leadership.

His message is one that applies to anyone who leads, whatever his or her title.

BEYOND CONTRIBUTION

Life is not infinite. There are limited hours in the day. We all must choose, whenever possible, where to invest our energy. Where will we realize the greatest impact?

Most people who serve as leaders at some point ask themselves, "How can I contribute?" Many of us were raised with the belief that simply being a consumer of the world's resources isn't enough. To achieve deeper fulfillment, we must contribute, as well.

Fortunately, opportunities to give present themselves every day. But the most effective of those among us who act as leaders realize that a better question to ask ourselves is "How can I *best* contribute?"

Serving in any way is admirable—and it is important that we are willing to do so. But when we have unique skills and passions, we can have an even greater impact if we look at the ways we can contribute that will do the most good.

GIVING IS A GIFT THAT GIVES BACK

My favorite bookstore in Denver is The Tattered Cover in Cherry Creek.

Not long ago, I was waiting in the checkout line with a few purchases. In front of me were a bunch of inner-city kids touring The Tattered Cover as part of a summer class. To encourage them to read, the store had given each a gift certificate to use toward buying books. I thought it was a great idea.

The little girl directly in front of me arrived at the counter with three books she hoped to buy with her certificate. I could sense her nervousness. The cashier totaled the books, and it turned out the little girl didn't have nearly a big enough certificate to buy all three. She quickly decided to set one aside. On the second tally, the two remaining books were still too much.

At this point, people behind me in line were wondering what was holding up the line. Even the cashier with the sunny disposition was getting a little antsy. Worst of all, it appeared the little girl was about to give up trying to buy any books.

Acting on impulse, I quickly reached into my pocket for a five-dollar bill. "Will this allow her to get both books?" I asked. The five just covered the difference, with pennies left over. The little girl glanced up shyly and muttered, "Thank you." The woman behind me threw her arms around me and gave me a big hug. "You've restored my faith in human nature!" she exclaimed.

I share this story not to point out what a nice guy I can be. Actually, I am ashamed of all the opportunities I've had to give that I didn't see or seize.

I tell you this story because I realized later that it was the best $5 I spent that month. I didn't give the young girl money because of my need for recognition. I simply did it to help a little girl who I felt would benefit from owning and reading good books.

The incident reminded me that we can't give to others without being affected positively ourselves. And this is the secret of giving: *When you make the world better for others, you make the world better for yourself.*

For the twenty-odd years I've worked in leadership development, I've observed that giving—being of service—can be the most overlooked aspect of leadership, whatever your title. Usually, when we think of leadership we think of performance, effectiveness, and results. But those critical aspects of leadership shine all the more brightly when they coexist with giving, service, and contribution. Together, they help to bring the best and highest from each of us.

LEADERSHIP ACTION POINTS

PRACTICE GIVING WITHOUT RECOGNITION

True giving is about what one contributes rather than what one receives. While leaders often get recognition for their service, that is not the objective in serving. Find a way to contribute to a colleague or customer anonymously. Sometimes serving anonymously is a great way to learn how to go beyond simply giving.

DETERMINE HOW YOU CAN *BEST* CONTRIBUTE

Few of us have the luxury to do only what we are best at or would like to do. But that shouldn't prevent us from determining how we can best contribute our time, talents, and knowledge.

How can you best contribute to others?

GIVE AS A FAMILY

By taking on a project together as a family, family members can both spend quality time together and work to help others. Every community has a hospital, school, and/or retirement community. Finances are often limited, and volunteers are usually welcomed. Look around for the individuals and organizations that need your help.

PART III

MAKING A POSITIVE DIFFERENCE

LEAVING A LEADERSHIP LEGACY

Let us endeavor to live that when we come to die even the undertaker will be sorry.
—MARK TWAIN

DIFFERENCE MAKERS

Everyone matters. Everyone makes a difference.

The cynic might argue that he or she could choose to be neutral, to make neither a positive nor a negative difference. In practice, that just ain't so.

Have you recently encountered a person who didn't seem engaged? Perhaps he or she seemed wrapped up in their own private world, leaving you with the impression that you weren't important enough to gain admittance. Don't you hate being ignored that way?

If you were to press that person, he might tell you he was simply being "neutral." He might not have been as helpful or interested in you as he could have been, but he wasn't doing you any harm.

To me, that kind of rationalization is akin to the bystander at a mugging who chooses not to get involved. The fact is, he *has* acted, in this case negatively, by *not* getting involved.

In practical terms, neutrality is a myth.

The greatest insult in business or in life is indifference. You can't engage the world in a meaningful way by being "neutral." The perception of those around you will be that they don't matter enough for you to engage with them.

My point is that *everyone* makes a difference. The choice we all have is whether we want to make a *positive* difference or a *negative* one.

At the end of the day, have you made a positive or a negative difference with the people in your life?

- Your client or customer, who was in a pinch and needed immediate attention?
- Your son or daughter, who wanted you to read to him or her when you were busy preparing for the next business day?
- The stranger on the way to work who said good morning to you without getting a response?

The positive or negative impact you have on each person above varies only in magnitude. The principle is the same. When you choose not to make a positive difference, you almost always make a negative one.

Our actions and behaviors matter more than we realize. People who act as leaders understand that *everything* they do—and do not do—is significant. The first job of those who act as leaders—whatever their title—is to convince others of the significance of their actions.

What we choose to do can improve, even if only in some small way, the quality of another person's day or life.

ACTIVITY VS. ACCOMPLISHMENT

When a salesperson perfunctorily calls on a customer account to tell them about a product or service, he or she is engaging in *activity*, but usually to no great effect. But when he or she *shows* that account how to use his product or service to increase revenue, he is *accomplishing* something.

Managing people in order to ensure that they do what they're supposed to do is a necessary *activity*. Taking time to lead them to new levels of success is a significant *accomplishment*.

What percentage of your day is made up of activity, as opposed to accomplishment?

Accomplishment begins with a simple commitment each day to improve the lives of those you interact with. That doesn't necessarily mean you should intervene in a personal family matter, but it might mean you provide encouragement to someone who is discouraged, or brighten someone's day with a kind word or compliment.

Who wants to go through life without having any genuine impact—without interacting with or positively affecting others? Who wants to spend eight to ten hours a day on a job that doesn't matter to them, feeling as if they've accomplished little at the end of the day?

RÉSUMÉ SKILLS VS. LEADERSHIP SKILLS

Our culture is obsessed with success. We assume that if we

become really good at what we do, we will earn material benefits and accolades. But Richard Halverson, former chaplain of the U.S. Senate, points out that our goal in life shouldn't be just to "be good," but rather to "be good *for something.*"

If that "something" is limited to merely personal success, our impact on the world around us will be limited. In other words, don't confuse résumé skills with leadership skills.

Résumé	Legacy
What you've accomplished	What you've contributed
Results	Relationships
The money you've made	The difference you've made
The impression you leave	The impact you have
Your career	Your organization, family, and community
Self-improvement	Helping others improve

Are you building a strong résumé or preparing to leave a lasting legacy?

BELIEVING IN A BETTER WORLD

According to Barna Research, only one of four Americans has a life philosophy.

Fewer still have a notion about the kind of legacy they want to leave.

Philosophy—literally, a "love of wisdom"—answers the big questions that underlie all the little questions of life. The best philosophy affects not just what we think or believe but how we behave and what we do. Philosophy seeks to answer the question "How should we live?" What I've found over the years is that *why* we live is usually more important than *how*.

In his book *Reality and the Vision*, author Calvin Miller writes that there are several reasons he reads science-fiction writer Ray Bradbury. After reciting them, he concludes, "Finally, I read and re-read Bradbury because I need to believe in a better world." I think that is exactly what motivates and drives each of us when we act as leaders, whether in our work lives or our personal lives. That is true whether we lead from the bottom up and shun publicity and titles, or from the top down.

RESPONDING TO DIFFICULTIES

Years ago, as a college student, I heard a speaker say something that has stuck with me ever since: Everybody hurts. No matter how successful a person is, life can be painful. Personal setbacks are a daily occurrence. We are continually challenged and confronted with problems at work and in other areas of our lives. If you aren't experiencing challenges or difficulties at present, remember that you have in the past and you certainly will again.

Foundation-shaking change, increased competition, displacement, diminishing resources, and uncertainty about tomorrow are part of "business as usual" in the corporate world as well. Even those companies that are successful today realize (or should) that the distance from being a supernova to being extinct can be very short indeed.

Not all people who face challenges and difficulties admit to them. Too often we try to deal with difficulty by ignoring it or anesthetizing it with activity. The healthiest companies and individuals see challenges for what they are, accept them, and work to solve them.

People who act as leaders, whether they have a title or not, in some measure serve as merchants of hope. This doesn't mean that they try to gloss over the difficulties that are being faced. Rather, they deal with them. People who lead show us that the greatest satisfaction often comes from meeting challenges head-on. They have the ability to focus on what's *right* and on overcoming what's wrong. They help to find the pony in the pile of manure.

THE LEADER NEXT DOOR

> You have within you more resources of energy than have ever been tapped, more talent than has ever been exploited, more strength than has ever been tested, more to give than you have ever given.
>
> —JOHN GARDNER, former Secretary of
> Health, Education and Welfare

Tony was at an awkward time in his life: A shy and self-conscious fifteen-year-old, he had just spent three years sitting on the bench of his junior high basketball team. His coach, who also coached the baseball team, discouraged Tony from coming out for the baseball team, to save him the embarrassment of being cut. Tony took his advice. His dream of athletic achievement had seemingly come to an end.

Then one morning the doorbell rang. When Tony answered the door, he found his fifty-something-year-old neighbor, Frank

Wethern, standing there. Tony was about to turn to get his parents when Frank said, "No, I'm not here to see your parents, Tony. I'm here to see you. I'm going for a run. I wondered if you'd like to join me."

It was 1973, the spring after Frank Shorter had won the Olympic marathon that helped to launch the running boom in the United States. But running was still a relatively obscure sport and not something most kids did, at least not the cool or popular ones. Although Tony didn't particularly want to go, for some reason he said yes.

They ran to the high school track. Frank used his old stopwatch to time Tony for four laps around the dusty oval. It took him eight minutes, "just twice as long as Roger Bannister," as Frank explained. As they walked home, Tony thought about a human being breaking the four-minute mile. It seemed impossible.

But Frank wasn't through. He suggested that Tony could be a pretty good miler, and maybe even break four minutes himself someday. He encouraged his young neighbor to go out for the track team.

Coincidentally, the next Monday at school, Mr. Kafka, the track coach, pulled Tony aside in the hallway and told him there was a track meet the next day. "How'd you like to run the mile?" the coach inquired.

Tony came in last place in his first race. But he kept at it. And he got better and better. In fact, Tony Schiller went on to enjoy a 33-year career as one of America's top endurance athletes. He has won over 170 races, including 78 triathlons. At

47, he remains a contender against top athletes half his age. In the over-40 category, he has won six national and five world titles. He has also become a motivational speaker, and the creator and director of the MiracleKids Triathlon, a major fundraiser for kids with cancer.

"I've often thought of how different my life would have turned out if Frank had simply jogged by the house that morning, as he had always done," Tony reflected. "After all, he claims it had always been his belief that, unless invited, one should never stick his nose into other people's business. But on that day . . . he felt a strong impulse to reach out to me. . . . As is so often the case, the simple gesture done at just the right moment can be life-changing. It was for me that day. Those four laps gave a very troubled teen's life a completely new direction. And so I will always be grateful to Frank Wethern for having broken his own rule by sticking his nose into my business. For some reason, he and Coach Kafka were on some kind of psychic karma. They both not only reached out to me at my biggest moment of need, they did it by zeroing right in on where my life-gift sat waiting to be discovered. I'm convinced the gift would have sat that way, too—at least for a very long time—had either one turned away from the urge to help me."

Both of these men left a lasting legacy to Tony Schiller and to the world.

WHY NOT *YOU*?

My friend Gloria had been battling a rare form of cancer. She called me six months before she passed away to ask me to be a pallbearer at her funeral. Of course, I said yes. But I hoped it would be a long time before I had to make good on my promise. That did not turn out to be the case.

Glo was a vivacious human being who faced more adversity than almost any person I've known. Despite that, I had never heard her complain.

At her funeral, an old friend of hers recalled talking to Glo about her illness. Glo's cancer was very painful, and she struggled back from the brink of death on several occasions. Her friend, expressing her own sense of frustration, told Gloria, "There are so many evil people in the world. Why aren't they suffering like this? Why you, Gloria?"

Gloria responded with the same undefeatable spirit she had lived with her entire life. She said, "Why not me? I have faith and I'm tough. I can take it."

This kind of mental and spiritual toughness are signatures of people who act as leaders in life. They don't tend to worry or wonder about why bad things happen to them. Instead, they accept and deal with the cards they are dealt. They are able to embrace challenge because they're confident they possess the attitude and skills needed to succeed.

WHAT IS YOUR LEGACY?

When I first visited the big island of Hawaii, I was particularly impressed with the volcanic rock fields the road we traveled on cut through from the airport to Kona. The road was lined with hundreds of white stones, which had been carefully placed in stark contrast against the black rock of the lava field. These stones spelled out the names of people, and often the date they had passed through: "Bob & Sally, 11/88," "Jean, Spring Break '91." It reminded me of what so often happens when graffiti artists assault bridges and water towers with their public art.

All of us want our lives to be significant, to believe we'll do something, somehow, that will be remembered. Sometimes leaving a legacy can be as simple as placing stones in the lava. But for most of us, the best evidence we can leave that we passed through life is to lead whenever we can. Leadership isn't a mysterious art practiced by only a select few. It is the daily response of every man and woman who wishes to make a positive difference in the world and make it a little bit better place as a result of their efforts.

In my experience, the marks in life we leave—our legacies—are most often left not in stone and steel, in history and politics, or poetry and literature, but in the lives of other people.

MASTERING LEADERSHIP

A student once asked a martial arts master how long it would take him to master the martial art he was learning.

The master replied, "How long do you expect to live?"

Mastering leadership, too, is a lifelong process. All of us can learn to lead better; none of us ever truly masters leadership. When it comes to leadership, we're all WIPs—works in progress.

Each of our lives is a leadership lab. We don't need a title, or an organization, to lead. What we need is nothing more nor less than a burning desire to make a positive difference and an awareness of the opportunities to lead that present themselves each day—at work, at home, with our friends and relatives, within our communities.

If each of us chose to lead at the right time in the right way, what might our companies be like? Our communities? Our world?

I hope that some of the ideas in this book will help you to make a positive difference.

—Mark Sanborn, CSP, CPAE

ABOUT THE AUTHOR

MARK SANBORN is an internationally acclaimed keynote speaker, bestselling author, and noted authority on leadership. He is the president of Sanborn & Associates, Inc., an idea lab dedicated to developing leaders in business and life. Mark has written numerous books, including the *Wall Street Journal* bestseller *The Fred Factor: How Passion in Your Work and Life Can Turn the Ordinary into the Extraordinary.*

Mark has presented over 2,000 speeches and seminars in every state and many foreign countries. He holds the Certified Speaking Professional (CSP) from the National Speakers Association and is a member of the exclusive Speakers Hall of Fame (CPAE). He is a past president of the National Speakers Association.

Mark's live presentations include:

High Impact Leadership
How the Best Get Better
You Don't Need a Title to Be a Leader
The Fred Factor: How to Make the Ordinary Extraordinary
The 10 Commandments of Customer Service

For more information, visit www.marksanborn.com or call Sanborn & Associates, Inc., at 800-650-3343.

For free leadership resources to complement this book, go to www.youdontneedatitle.com.

LEARN TO LEAD—OR LEAD BETTER!

BEGIN WITH A FREE AUDIO LESSON

Continue to develop your leadership skills. We have made the next step as simple and inexpensive as possible. It's FREE. Visit www.youdontneedatitle.com to take advantage of these free learning resources: an audio lesson with Mark Sanborn, a summary handout of the key principles of leadership, and a subscription to Leadership Lessons ezine.

ORDER LIVE OR DVD-BASED TRAINING TODAY

Mark's bestselling book *The Fred Factor* proves that you can learn a lot from a mailman! The book and message have become a business classic and you can train you and your team on the principles of Fred and his remarkable way of making the ordinary extraordinary. To order, go to www.fredfactor.com

To learn more about **LIVE** leadership training at your organization, go to www.youdontneedatitle.com or call 800-650-3343.

BRING MARK SANBORN TO YOUR ORGANIZATION!

Mark Sanborn is an award-winning speaker known for his dynamic presentation style. He provides audiences with actionable ideas and powerful insights on leadership, customer service, and motivation. Having Mark speak can make your next meeting or event extraordinary.

To bring Mark Sanborn to your organization, go to www.marksanborn.com or call 800-650-3343.